To: Tom & Patti
Hope you Enjoy.
Best Wishes
Dellert McDonald

FAILURE IS NOT AN OPTION

*Delbert McDougal,
A Developer's Unconventional Wisdom*

By Tony Privett

*Many of life's failures are
people who did not realize
how close they were to success
when they gave up.*

- Thomas Edison (1847-1931)

First Edition

Copyright © 2007 Legacy Editions, a division of Historical Publishing Network

All rights reserved. No part of this book may be reproduced in any form or by any means, electronic or mechanical, including photocopying, without permission in writing from the publisher. All inquiries should be addressed to Historical Publishing Network, 11555 Galm Road, Suite 100, San Antonio, Texas, 78254. Phone (800) 749-9790.

ISBN: 9781893619746

Library of Congress Card Catalog Number: 2007934049

Failure is Not an Option: Delbert McDougal, A Developer's Unconventional Wisdom

author: Tony Privett

Historical Publishing Network

president: Ron Lammert
administration: Donna M. Mata, Evelyn Hart
book sales: Dee Steidle
production: Colin Hart, Craig Mitchell, Charles A. Newton III

TABLE OF CONTENTS

		Page
FOREWORD by Bob Knight		6
INTRODUCTION		8
CHAPTER 1	*The cotton patch, 1937-1955*	10
CHAPTER 2	*GE brings good things to life, 1957-1982*	13
CHAPTER 3	*Starting a new business, 1982-1984*	21
CHAPTER 4	*Hard business lessons, 1984-1990*	33
CHAPTER 5	*Changes in the marketplace, 1990 – 1999*	43
CHAPTER 6	*Reclaiming a neighborhood, 1999 – 2003*	53
CHAPTER 7	*Redevelopment lessons, 2003 - 2006*	69
CHAPTER 8	*Overton Park, 2007 and beyond*	73
CHAPTER 9	*Passing on the secrets*	81
AFTERWORD	*Reflections of the author*	86
ACKNOWLEDGEMENTS		88

FOREWORD

By Bob Knight

When I first came to Lubbock, Texas, to coach the men's basketball team at Texas Tech University, I was coming not as a complete stranger to the people who lived here or the characteristics inherent in its people.

My Dad grew from childhood to adulthood in east central Oklahoma and so was a product of this same southwestern part of the United States where I had come to coach basketball. He was nine years old before Oklahoma had reached statehood and my Dad maintained a lifetime pride in the things he had learned as a youngster growing up in an agricultural environment in the southwestern United States.

From him I learned about perhaps the two most important ingredients in life; honesty and a willingness to work and do whatever it took in terms of effort to be successful.

Anytime that I would complain about things or cry about something to my Dad, until the day he passed away when I was twenty-nine years old, he would always ask me, "Did I ever tell you the story about chopping cotton for 25 cents a day when I was growing up and 90 degrees was a cool day?" We eventually both got to laughing every time he brought that up because I could tell the story better than he could.

Long before coming to West Texas I was very proud of the fact that at least to some degree the pioneer spirit, the fierce independence, the willingness to take a chance with nothing to depend on but your own abilities, resources and perseverance that led to people settling and developing the southwestern United States was a part of my heritage through Dad.

Not long after coming to Lubbock I met a man who reminded me of the independence, the honesty, and the work ethic that I had seen and watched in my Dad.

That man's name was Delbert McDougal.

I have always been intrigued by people that I think are special because of what they have accomplished and what they have been able to do with their lives. Delbert's incredible success in business, the community and life itself was long established before I came to Lubbock.

I decided that I wanted to find out as much about this man as I could and why he was able to do not only what he had done with his own life and that of his family, but what he had done for an entire community as well.

One of the first things I learned about Delbert was that he was a product of the same hot summers, agricultural background and cotton fields in west Texas that my Dad had been a part of in east central Oklahoma. I further learned that Delbert had done his work with a hoe in his hand, chopping cotton for 45 cents an hour, as opposed to my Dad at least according to my Dad, which I always doubted to a degree, getting 25 cents a day.

Be that as it may, it is an indication that when Delbert was chopping cotton he was a lot sharper in terms of negotiating his wages than my Dad had been.

As a ten-year-old boy I am sure that Delbert had no thought about the incredible heritage that he had not only from his family but from all those people who had the courage and the independence to pack up everything they owned in Alabama or Tennessee or any of the Midwestern states and move westward to a vast and unsettled, wild and dangerous part of America.

Forty years later as an adult, Delbert was the personification of those characteristics—honesty, integrity, devotion to family, and work ethic—that he had inherited as a young boy. As I write this, Delbert's companies have developed $400 million worth of commercial and residential property and have listed or sold more than $1.5 billion worth of homes and commercial property. How did all of this get started?

It got started when a nineteen-year-old Delbert, after a year of business school, took a job with General Electric in an entry position as a stock clerk. There were no computers in 1957 so Delbert developed a process by which he used 3 x 5 cards to keep track of the thousands of appliances constantly arriving and leaving the large warehouse where he was in charge of inventory.

Starting at the very bottom in an entry-level position in the commercial giant that was General Electric is an early example of Delbert simply following those characteristics of the pioneer spirit of independence, courage, and a determination to succeed. He didn't ask General Electric for a job nor did he ask about pay raises and promotions. He simply asked for a chance.

From that chance with General Electric to the present, he has done more for the economic growth of West Texas in general and the City of Lubbock in particular than all other entities combined.

If Edna Ferber had wanted to write a real life story on the history of economic growth in West Texas, her book *Giant* would have been about Delbert McDougal, for this man of Scotch pioneer ancestry is the West Texas Giant of our times.

Bob Knight
Head Basketball Coach
Texas Tech University

INTRODUCTION

Chopping weeds in a cotton patch on long, hot West Texas summer days for forty-five cents an hour will set an indelible benchmark for hard work in a young man's mind.

This early lesson is how a ten-year-old boy named Delbert McDougal was introduced to the workforce. McDougal's family income almost totally revolved around the area farmers in Smyer, Texas, a tiny agricultural community in the southern plains of West Texas.

After graduating from high school, working at a variety of jobs, and completing a year of college business courses in 1956, McDougal went to work for General Electric. He took an entry-level position known as a stock card clerk. In this position, he was a human computer, using 3 x 5 cards to keep up with thousands of appliances constantly arriving and leaving a large warehouse.

Twenty five years later, McDougal had worked his way up the ladder with a string of promotions, and managed the sales and operations of a large territory in Texas and New Mexico for GE. He turned down more than one opportunity to transfer to a major market, because he didn't want to trade the quality of life he and his family enjoyed in Lubbock.

But Delbert also had another interest that kept him from continuing his climb up the corporate ladder. He had a vision to create his own housing company. He left General Electric with a good understanding of business, a little money in the bank, and a strong will to succeed.

Over the next quarter of a century, McDougal built a multi-million dollar apartment, property development, construction, and realty company. The McDougal Companies built or purchased more than five thousand apartments in five West Texas cities, and currently manages more than five thousand apartments in twelve Texas cities. His companies have developed more than $400 million in commercial and residential property, and have listed or sold more than $1.5 billion in homes and commercial property.

Home to the McDougal Companies is Lubbock, a city located in north west Texas with more than two hundred thousand residents. The city is a regional retail center, and its economic bases are driven by agriculture, a large medical community, and Texas Tech University. Adjacent to the University is an historic neighborhood known as Overton. It was on this tract of land sandwiched between Texas Tech and downtown Lubbock, where Lubbock's first housing neighborhood was created. More than sixty years later, this same neighborhood is where Delbert and his wife Carolyn began their apartment business.

In later years, Overton became divided into North and South Overton, as residents wanted to establish separate neighborhood identities. North Overton was home to many Tech students and young families, due to its proximity to the campus and central location for jobs.

As his apartment holdings in the area grew in the 1970s and '80s, many rental properties in North Overton were purchased by out-of-town owners. McDougal watched with concern as a growing urban blight of deteriorating properties and spiraling crime overran the once proud neighborhood.

After many years of meetings with business and political leaders who sought to solve the North Overton problem, McDougal asked company employee Jerry Roberson to quietly research the ownership and value of each piece of property. In spite of warnings and skepticism from community leaders, banks, and industry peers, Delbert McDougal announced in 1999 that he was going to redevelop the entire 325 acres without public assistance.

In 2007, just eight years after his daring move, McDougal has substantially completed the successful redevelopment of the area renamed as Overton Park.

The centerpieces of the project are a luxury hotel and conference center, quality retail shopping, restaurants, and a mixed-use residential and retail complex named The Centre at Overton Park.

In the span of eight years, what was valued at $28 million, will likely reach $700 million on the tax roll by 2009.

During that same period, crime in the area dropped significantly. Many low income residents who were trapped in a dangerous neighborhood are now enjoying a quality of life they never believed possible. The turnaround of North Overton has been called the largest privately funded urban renewal project in America.

How did McDougal accomplish this large and complex project in such a short time?

The lessons to be learned from McDougal's business successes are measured beyond the company's gross earnings, property values, or even the success of the North Overton transformation.

Delbert McDougal's leadership embodies the core American values of hard work, honest business dealings, fair treatment of employees, and a strong commitment to family and community. These are the qualities once prized by American business, and too often abandoned by the short term profit focus of today's corporate executives.

With a keen understanding of the housing business, shrewd negotiating skills, and a tenacious problem-solving approach, McDougal looked for opportunities where others saw problems. He found a way to succeed when unexpected hurdles seemed insurmountable to those around him.

While others look for ways to get out of a deal when it runs into unforeseen problems, Delbert finds solutions and forges ahead. Through it all, McDougal built a strong family business while giving generously of his time and money to his community.

Delbert McDougal is a hard-nosed businessman with a big heart. His ability to succeed while caring for the needs of his customers is a model for any business person, from the sole proprietor to the corporate president.

As McDougal Company employees, family members, and friends readily attest, once Delbert McDougal makes up his mind to do something, failure is not an option.

Chester, Alda, Delbert, and Harvey McDougal, c. 1957.

CHAPTER 1

THE COTTON PATCH, 1937-1955

Delbert McDougal didn't exactly grow up in a privileged childhood. He was born at home on January 29, 1937, and grew up in the small West Texas town of Smyer with his older brother Harvey. Chester and Alda McDougal raised their sons in their early years in a building formerly used as a bunk house by the Santa Fe Railroad.

"Actually, we raised both boys in church," Alda McDougal said. "We were pretty much there every time the doors opened."

Both parents worked six days a week. Reflecting on his childhood, Delbert remembers, "We didn't have any money, but we weren't aware of it. We always had what we needed, and stayed busy working."

Delbert's father Chester, "Check" to his friends, worked for the Santa Fe Railroad for a number of years as a section hand. He left the railroad and opened his own mechanic's shop in a garage next to their small frame house. Check worked on irrigation motors and tractors for the farmers in the small farming community. The family's livelihood was almost totally dependent on Smyer's agricultural economy.

"I saw my first building project up close when Dad built a building to serve as the United States Post Office for Smyer," Delbert remembers. "Dad constructed a 600-square-foot building on our property next to his mechanic's shop. He leased it back to the government for $25 per month. My

Mother worked at the post office for about twenty-five years."

"I learned how to work hard from my folks, from Monday through Saturday," said Delbert.

Delbert and Harvey worked in the cotton fields in the summer, as soon as they were tall enough to hold a hoe. In West Texas, this work was known as "chopping cotton," even though it was the weeds that were cut.

Delbert has not forgotten his first salary.

"I made 45 cents an hour," he said. "They paid my older brother Harvey 55 cents an hour, because they rationalized that I was younger and couldn't do as much work. I don't remember ever being out-worked by my brother, however. Mom would usually work with us, to make sure we did a good job and keep any brotherly arguments from escalating into a fight."

The McDougals would hoe cotton all summer, starting at 5:00 a.m. They stopped about 3:00 when it got brutally hot. In the fall, Delbert and Harvey would again join their mom in the fields after school, to pull cotton and drag their harvest in long, heavy sacks until dark.

After the cotton harvest was complete, Delbert would help his father clean engine parts in the shop after school. The majority of his repair business was farm equipment.

While he worked hard from a very early age, Delbert admits he was a mischievous boy.

"I got into trouble a number of times," he said. "I guess I inherited my dad's pugnacious personality, and did a lot of fighting growing up.

"My brother and I fought, as brothers will do. But if one of us got in a disagreement with another boy, we came to each other's defense.

"I also remember 'playing army' one afternoon with a few guys. We imagined the local drugstore was the enemy fort and shot at it with our BB guns. The owner walked out the front door and started yelling at us, so we made a hasty retreat. By the time I got home, he was already there talking to my Dad.

"While I wasn't court-martialed, I did have to pay $300 for my share of the broken windows. It took all the money I had saved, plus several more months to pay off my foolishness. But I learned there were consequences to bad decisions. It turned out to be one of the best lessons I ever learned."

In small towns like Smyer, kids had to be creative to get into trouble. Delbert and his friends would sometimes prowl around after dark and turn over a few outdoor toilets.

"One time we got word that the local grocery store owner, was bragging he was going to hide in the outhouse and catch whoever was turning over the outhouse next to his store," Delbert said. "We knew he was planning to burst out and chase us down when he heard us walking up. So we hid and watched him go into the outhouse, then we let him wait there awhile. Then, we snuck up very slowly and quietly and threw a rope around the building to prevent him from getting out, pulled it tight, and turned the building over with him in it."

"All in all, it was a pretty typical small town American childhood. We didn't have any money to buy beer from a bootlegger, and there weren't any drugs that I was aware of. Like most boys, we would get some cigarettes and try to smoke them because it seemed like a manly thing to do.

"But I was broken of the nicotine habit early on. I had been bugging my granddad to let me try some of his Brown Mule chewing tobacco, but he wouldn't do it. One day, he cut a plug of tobacco for himself, and I grabbed it and ran. The problem was, he didn't chase me. I put it in

Brothers Harvey (left) and Delbert, c. 1942.

my mouth and swallowed quite a bit of it. I was sick for three days, and haven't chewed since. We should try that approach with kids today."

"Delbert also threw a snowball through the school superintendent's window," his mother Alda remembered. "I think he was surprised that it broke the window, but Check got after him with his belt anyway.

"All in all, Delbert and Harvey were both good boys."

Delbert met his future wife Carolyn Ratliff at church in nearby Levelland, a city with several thousand residents.

"Our first official date was after church on Sunday night in January 1954," Carolyn said. "Delbert would show up about the time church let out on Sunday night and mingle with the church crowd on the lawn. My mom thought Delbert had gone to church and let me go out with him. My folks liked Delbert from the start."

Carolyn and Delbert had much in common. She also grew up in a tiny neighboring community, named Whitharral.

"My grandfather owned a cotton gin," Carolyn said. "We lived in a cluster of houses close to the gin. I had 24 cousins, and 22 of them lived within a block of each other.

"Dad hauled wheat in Kansas in the summer when the gin wasn't operating. We moved to nearby Levelland when I was in the eighth grade. Dad worked as a mechanic, and Mom worked in grocery stores."

After graduating from Smyer High School in 1955, Delbert worked as a butcher's helper at Jordan Wholesale Meats in Muleshoe, a neighboring community. That lasted for six months.

Delbert and Carolyn dated for a while, but their relationship was interrupted by Delbert's move to Lubbock to look for work and continue his education.

McDougal felt the lure of opportunity in the big city, and left the butcher shop to move 70 miles to the county seat, with a population of 96,000 and home to Texas Tech University. He found work at the Shook Tire Company, as a retread machine operator. Noting the inherent danger in this position, Delbert was proud to have managed to leave the company after three months with all his fingers still attached.

But the enterprising young man was looking for something better. He found an opportunity

Delbert, 1959.

in the financial field, though it also was a short-term position.

"I got my first experience with finances when I worked as a collection agent for General Finance Company," Delbert noted. "This was a small loan company in downtown Lubbock. I quickly learned that it was not wise to loan money at high interest rates to people who could not afford to pay them back. It was not a good way for a young collection agent to make any money."

In 1956, Delbert furthered his education at Draughan's Business College, located in downtown Lubbock. He completed a year's worth of courses in General Business. He was nineteen years old.

"As I pondered my next career move, I was reminded by my Dad to get a good job and keep it," Delbert said. "Dad was definitely from the old school. He cautioned me a number of times about not going into debt and not buying anything I couldn't pay cash for. To the best of my knowledge, he borrowed very little money."

"I owe so much to my parents. They gave me a strong work ethic and values to deal honestly with other people. I learned to treat people with respect. These qualities are the foundation of any success I've had."

"To this day, I'm not happy if I'm not working. And I am living proof of the fact that you don't have to come from a wealthy family to be successful."

CHAPTER 2

GE BRINGS GOOD THINGS TO LIFE, 1957-1982

Delbert, Carolyn, Mike, and Marc, c. 1968.

After graduating high school and completing a year of business college, Delbert McDougal went to work for General Electric's major appliance division in Lubbock as a stock card clerk. He learned of the position through the Texas Employment Agency, and started work in the summer of 1957.

It was Delbert's job to keep an inventory of all the company's appliances in the Lubbock warehouse. That included hundreds of refrigerators, ranges, washers, dryers, and televisions. Delbert used color-coded cards to keep up with all the varieties and styles of products, acting as a human computer. Each variation of product was noted by a different color. For example, there were different colored cards for refrigerators with doors that opened to the left, and those that opened to the right.

His starting salary was $45 dollars a week.

In April 1959, after nearly two years with the company, McDougal was promoted to Dallas in a management-training program. This position consisted of processing appliance orders for delivery to new construction homes and apartments. He coordinated deliveries with job superintendents to assure that construction progress was not held up.

While in Dallas, Delbert worked for Vin Sweeney, a man who would have a strong influence on him for his twenty-five years with General Electric. Vin remembered the young man's strong drive as a young employee.

"Delbert was the best stock card clerk in America," stated Sweeney. "It was unbelievable how much effort he put into an entry level job. He kept up with a large warehouse of appliances, using cards. Occasionally, someone in the warehouse would say they were out of stock of an item that Delbert showed on his card that we had. He would simply go into the warehouse and look until he found it. He was very organized and confident."

Chapter 2 ◆ 13

"He was only twenty years old at the time, but I'd never seen a young man take his job so seriously. So I moved him to Dallas to be an order service clerk. He did a great job there, too."

McDougal was on his way up. After only five months in Dallas, he was promoted to manage GE's El Paso operation in December 1959. This was a big step for a twenty-year-old. His duties included management of appliance services, wholesale and retail parts departments, ordering and warehousing of all inventory, pricing of all orders submitted by customers and GE sales personnel, customer credit, and assisting the sales staff to assure positive customer service.

"When I promoted Delbert to take over the El Paso market," Sweeney remembered, "he had two difficult jobs. First, he took over an area that needed much work. Second, the manager in El Paso was expected to be the Juarez tour director for all GE regional and national managers who came to El Paso. "

Juarez was a hopping border town, located just across the Rio Grande River from El Paso. During this time, it was a popular place for men who liked to chase the night life. McDougal took many a group of traveling GE executives to Juarez for a night in "boys' town."

Before he moved to El Paso, Delbert and Carolyn had maintained occasional contact. He would see her when he went back to Lubbock, but they didn't describe their relationship as serious during this period. When he moved to El Paso, Delbert was surprised to learn that Carolyn's grandmother lived very close to the General Electric office in El Paso.

They began to date again, this time getting more serious. Delbert drove back and forth from El Paso to Levelland to see Carolyn on weekends. He would often leave Carolyn's house about midnight and arrive in El Paso Monday morning in time to go to work.

"After deciding that the drives were killing me," Delbert said, "I asked Carolyn's father for permission to marry her one evening in their living room. I'll never forget his answer.

❖

Carolyn hold's Delbert's "Mr. Football" trophy, c. 1955.

Mr. Ratliff said, "Well, let's just get out in the back yard and get it over with."

"That was a great relief," said Delbert. "I expected him to throw me out the front door."

Delbert and Carolyn were married on April 2, 1961.

After moving to El Paso, his new bride learned about the "tour director" part of Delbert's job, hosting company representatives on evenings in Juarez, and its well-deserved reputation for wild times.

"After Delbert came in from a late night in Juarez with some managers," Carolyn remembered, "I told him that we were a married couple now, and that if he wanted to go to Juarez to entertain company executives, that was just fine. But I was going to go with him on future trips. From that point on, we entertained in Juarez together."

It was during this time in El Paso that Delbert started working directly with builders and began to learn the industry from the inside. He established an additional customer base of builders for GE, outside the normal sales department efforts. His ability to attract more customers for the company led to his being offered a full time job representing GE to builders and other retail dealers in Southern New Mexico.

"Delbert had more drive than anyone I ever managed," said his former supervisor Vin Sweeney. "When he was in El Paso, Delbert didn't have a big enough warehouse to handle all the appliances he was selling. We started storing merchandise in Dallas for the El Paso region."

"One time, our Dallas crew didn't do a good job of loading a box car of appliances when they shipped them to El Paso, and much of the load arrived damaged. Delbert was furious when he saw the shipment. It only took one blistering phone call to the warehouse manager to make sure that problem never happened again."

During those early years in El Paso, money was still tight for the young married couple.

"My brother-in-law had an illness in 1964, and wasn't expected to live long," said Delbert. "He was in Baylor Hospital in Dallas. We'd recently been blessed with our first son, Marc. We didn't have much money. We needed some extra cash so Carolyn could travel to Dallas to be with her brother. I went to a bank and borrowed $100 and I paid it back with $10 monthly payments.

Shortly thereafter, in 1965 Delbert went against his father's advice, borrowing $14,500 to build his family a small home across the street from the Baptist church they attended.

The McDougals stayed in El Paso six years. Before they left, their second son Mike was born.

Delbert continued to have great success with the company. In April 1966, they were elated to be offered the General Electric district manager's job in Lubbock. They were coming home.

"In Lubbock, my responsibility was to maintain and develop business relationships with the building industry in West Texas and Southern New Mexico, including the El Paso market," Delbert said.

"I established warehouses in Midland, Amarillo, El Paso, and Lubbock. Working closely with builders during these years gave me great insight into the building industry."

He would use this insight to great advantage years later in building his own business.

When the McDougals came back to Lubbock, they bought a new house. The home had been built as a model home, to show off the latest in design and appliances. They loved the home, but there was one small problem. The builder used all gas appliances. This posed a problem for the local manager of the country's major electric appliance distributor, who happened to be Delbert's boss at GE.

To fix the problem, Delbert negotiated a deal with the builder to buy back all the gas appliances. Sparkling new GE electric appliances were brought in to replace the gas models.

As the boys got older, Delbert felt the need to expose them to outdoor sports. He started hunting and fishing, so he and Carolyn could take the boys on weekend outings. The family also developed its own daily routines.

Because the family works together, sons Marc and Mike refer to their parents as Delbert and Carolyn, rather than Mom and Dad.

"Regardless of how busy Delbert was," his youngest son Mike said, "we had dinner at 6:30 sharp every night. It didn't matter what you were doing, you had better be home at 6:30 for dinner. Often, Delbert would go back to the

Carolyn and Delbert in front of his first new car, a 1959 Ford Fairlane.

office after work, but he and Carolyn wanted the family to have dinner together every night.

"Breakfast was at 7:30 every morning. I knew that if I was on time for breakfast and dinner, I could avoid most of the trouble I saw Marc getting into."

DELBERT'S SALES SKILLS

In the early 1970s, GE changed its structure to include a competing brand, Hotpoint, to be sold in Texas under a Dallas manager with a separate sales force. Hotpoint was manufactured by General Electric, but made with fewer features and a lower cost.

Delbert was by nature very competitive, which served him well as he rose up in the GE sales ranks. Just because the company made money off Hotpoint, Delbert didn't like selling a lower quality line. He viewed Hotpoint with the same disdain he did all other competitors.

Vin Sweeney remembers one particular episode that illustrates Delbert's determination, when going after business against Hotpoint.

"One of Delbert's accounts in Midland, Texas, was the target of some very low pricing by the Hotpoint salesman," Sweeney said. "Delbert was not planning to lose the account, so he matched the Hotpoint bid in order to get the business. He was not authorized to do that, and I had to endure an earful from my boss over the incident."

"Delbert's rationale was that if he lost that order, the company would lose thousands of dollars in the future by his account's buying a lower cost product. I stood up for Delbert, and the order was delivered.

Vin Sweeney could see that Delbert had the drive and skills to go far with the company. In reflecting on his star performer, Vin noted that Delbert was a great salesman who developed friendships with most of his customers.

But if all else failed, Delbert could also be very forceful with his customers if they tried to tell him they were going to purchase another brand.

"One time, I saw Delbert get red-faced and furious with a prospective customer, who wouldn't be convinced to buy from him," Vin remembered.

"Delbert told this man that he was going to buy from GE, and that was that. And he got the order.

"Beyond his sales abilities," Vin noted, "Delbert is smart, honest, and loyal. I never saw anyone with as much drive as him, or with a more positive attitude. When he decided to do something, it happened.

"He was the best employee I ever had, and I directly or indirectly managed more than five hundred people in my career."

During the decade of the 1970s, Delbert turned down a number of promotion opportunities with General Electric, because he wanted to stay in Lubbock. He knew that meant his future with the company would be limited.

"My job forced me to travel quite a bit, and Carolyn had to assume a great deal of the parenting role in those years," Delbert said. "But we were raising our family in a wonderful town, and we were close to both our parents and extended families.

"We had no interest in moving to larger cities, bouncing around the country and uprooting our kids in order to climb the corporate ladder. In addition, our parents were aging and we wanted to stay close to them in their golden years."

One of the perks of his job was GE's travel rewards. Delbert and Carolyn would host good customers of GE to go on twelve-day trips around the world.

Delbert as a Smyer High School senior, c. 1955.

"Delbert and Carolyn probably wouldn't have spent their money for that kind of travel during those years," Marc said.

"They acquired a great love of travel from those trips, and also met a lot of successful business people in the process. I think it helped motivate them to build their own company and achieve that same level of success."

During Delbert's tenure with General Electric, the company was known as a great educator of people. He still has great respect for the company and acknowledges its influence on his subsequent success.

"Today most people think of Jack Welch, the high-profile former CEO, when they think of GE," Delbert said.

"In my time with the company, the focus was on our products. Now, companies often take on the face of their leader. While Mr. Welch certainly brought GE to another financial level, he was totally focused on the bottom line and didn't have the people skills, nor an appreciation for our employees like his predecessor.

"Reggie Jones, who held the top position before Jack Welch had tremendous respect from the employees. His management style was totally different from Welch's. The transition from Jones to Welch was difficult for those of us who grew up in the company under Jones' style.

"This is not to take anything away from what Jack Welch did for GE. He inherited a great company and he took it to a new level. But he was also difficult to talk to, and seemed to prefer to use intimidation in dealing with staff rather than take a true leadership role.

"A great deal of credit for that is due to Reggie Jones and the thousands of fine men and women throughout the country who built the company into the leading appliance company of its time. I will always be proud to have been a member of the General Electric team."

While succeeding as the Lubbock manager for GE, Delbert was also steadily working toward his plan of starting his own company. He felt that he could succeed in his own business beyond what was capable if he stayed with the appliance company.

"I knew that the older I got in corporate America, the more limited my growth would be," Delbert said. "That's not a slap on GE. It's just the way it works. They can bring in younger workers, who aren't making as much money, and are more willing to relocate."

Delbert began his journey into owning his own company in 1972 with the purchase of a sixteen-unit apartment building in Lubbock's Overton neighborhood named The Melrose.

THE HISTORY OF OVERTON

In 1907, Lubbock physician Dr. M. C. Overton bought 640 acres just west of the original Lubbock town site to build homes for the growing community.

The original deed to Overton was filed in Crosby County, because Lubbock did not have a courthouse at the time.

In Nan Overton West's biography of her father, *He Wore a Pink Carnation*, she notes that, "He planned to lay out streets in the Overton Addition, to set aside land for parks, and to sell houses and lots, making it the finest residential area in Lubbock, zoned to prevent any commercial intrusion. There were some who called the Overton Addition "Silk Stocking Row."

Less than a mile from the geographic center of Lubbock, North Overton is the oldest residential development in the city.

Left to right: A. J. "Jake" Ratliff, Mildred Ratliff, Carolyn Ratliff McDougal, Delbert McDougal, Alda McDougal, and Chester "Check" McDougal, April 2, 1961.

A proud father happy to be back in Lubbock with his sons, 1966.

At some point during the project, Dr. Overton ran into financial trouble and the property was foreclosed on by Republic Life Insurance in Dallas. Determined not to lose his dream, however, Dr. Overton attracted investors and bought it back.

By 1969, Overton was no longer silk stocking row, but was still a nice area to live. Many students rented there because of its proximity to the Texas Tech campus, and the homeowners were a mix of young couples buying their first home, and retired couples living in their last home.

"A friend of ours in the real estate business named George Bond asked us if we'd like to go in together to buy an apartment," Carolyn remembers. "Delbert had been around the apartment business, and knew a lot about it. George used his commission as his share of the down payment on The Melrose.

"We didn't have $10,000 for our down payment, and had to borrow it. Like Delbert, my family never bought anything unless they had the money in hand. I was terrified."

"I did all the leasing and cleaning, which I loved doing. That was invaluable experience for me. Our partner's wife worked in the school system. She kept the books for our partnership. "Delbert and George did all the maintenance after hours."

The McDougals managed their apartment complex with their partners for the next six years. In September of 1975, McDougal found another apartment to purchase.

Their first apartment was cash-flowing, but not by much. Delbert was able to find a local bank to loan him the down payment, and he made the purchase.

"The boys were 9 and 11 years old at this time," Carolyn said. "They were able to help with the cleaning, while I did the leasing and Delbert would handle the maintenance.

"Marc cleaned the living rooms and bedrooms, Mike would clean the kitchen, and I would clean the bathroom. The apartments were furnished, which made them harder to clean than if they were unfurnished. The boys were very involved with the business from that point on.

"Because of Delbert's work with GE," Carolyn said, "the boys grew up with all the latest appliances in the kitchen.

"These old apartments were unlike anything the boys had ever seen. I'll never forget the first one they helped me clean. I left Mike in the kitchen with his instructions, and went to the bathroom to start work.

"A few minutes later, Mike came in with a puzzled look on his face, wanting to know where the dishwasher was. He got his first experience in washing dishes without an electric dishwasher."

Lubbock's population began to grow to the south and west. Because of it's proximity to Texas Tech, Overton's population aged, and as the small homes became available, their new occupants increasingly were renters.

Throughout the 1970s, Delbert and Carolyn continued to purchase and manage apartments in central and south Lubbock, as an after-hours business.

"I'd set up an office in a newly acquired apartment, and would stay there until it was leased up," Carolyn said. "We'd normally have all our apartments filled up for the fall by July 15, mostly with Tech students.

"After acquiring our fourth apartment complex, the management duties required me to hire a little help. A couple of apartments had pools, and the boys had pool cleaning and upkeep added to their duties.

"We never paid our boys for their work at the apartments in the early years. We were barely paying all our bills and mortgages during this time. When they got to high school, we bought them used cars. They earned those cars by their work. We didn't "give" them anything. They worked after school and on Saturdays to help build this company."

The McDougal's sons Marc and Mike got their dad's feisty, competitive spirit, and he made sure they learned the value of hard work.

"I remember one time when I was in high school," Marc said. "I came home Saturday morning about 3:00, three hours past curfew. Dad got me up at 6:30 on Saturday morning, but didn't say a word about my missing curfew. He just handed me a list of things to do at one of the apartments. He told me when that list was finished to find him. The list took all morning, but I finished it and was looking forward to a nap.

"I found Dad and told him I was finished, and then he handed me another list of tasks at another apartment. When I finished that one, there was a third list of jobs. The lists finally stopped about 6:00 Saturday night. I remembered that the next time I considered staying out past curfew."

As the McDougal's apartment investments began to grow, they saw the possibility of building a business around the apartment industry. Because Delbert would not accept a transfer to the east coast, they would not be able to stay with GE indefinitely. His dream of running his own business was fast approaching.

LAS COLINAS

In 1980, Delbert decided to try a more ambitious plan. He and two friends built a 136-unit apartment complex in south Lubbock. They named it Las Colinas.

"This was the project that I believed would allow me to leave GE," Delbert said. "But interest rates began to skyrocket and the apartments weren't completed. I knew I had to stay with GE for a while longer."

This was a frightening time for Carolyn. She'd heard stories of fluctuations in apartment leasing, but this was different. She feared losing all the apartments they owned, because of this one deal that had gone sour.

"Delbert's position was that we were in the deal, and weren't going to back out of it," Carolyn said. "He was only focused on moving forward, to see it through to a positive outcome.

"Delbert is the eternal optimist. I am the worrier in the family.

Where the company began. The Melrose, his first apartment purchase, as it looks in 2007.

Las Colinas.

Delbert borrowed $3 million to build the Las Colinas apartments. They were paying prime plus-two percent for the loan. Before the project was completed, interest rates shot up to 21.5 percent.

"Shortly after we got our loan," Delbert said, interest rates began shooting up. By the time we got the apartments built, we were paying 23.5 percent interest. Even if we filled every apartment, we were going to lose a lot of money in a hurry at that rate!"

"Because of the interest rates, my partners became concerned about our ability to complete the project, which was about eighty percent finished," Delbert said.

"We met with Mr. Alan White, who was then president of Lubbock National Bank. He showed some confidence in us and helped us work out enough financing to get the project completed."

The Las Colinas partners were paying more than $80,000 a month in interest. Even though they could now complete the project, they weren't out of the woods.

Delbert was president of the local home builders association at the time, and he put together a bond issue for the local housing industry with a guaranteed ten percent interest rate.

Fortunately, there were numerous buyers willing to purchase apartments at that rate. Delbert found a buyer and just a few months after they were pondering financial ruin, the partners split a million-dollar profit on the complex.

Because of the tax law changes, as well as the real estate industry's problems, there was not much future for an investor to be involved in an apartment project. When the partners lost their tax advantage, there was no longer any reason for this partnership to stay in place.

"I never thought I'd lose money on this project, even when we were in financial straits," Delbert said. "Had I defaulted on this loan, I knew I'd never get another loan in Lubbock. That wasn't going to happen."

This deal was one of the turning points of McDougal's business education. He was paying historically high interest rates. If his bond plan hadn't worked, he would've moved to a private takeout.

"I felt I could have put together a group of investors to take the bank loan out," Delbert said. "I might have had to become an employee of the group, but I wouldn't have filed bankruptcy."

"Everything is not going to be an instant success. You have to have backup plans."

Delbert's backup plan worked. He sold Las Colinas, made a tidy profit, and was ready for his next move.

CHAPTER 3

STARTING A NEW BUSINESS, 1982-1984

After observing the industry from a supplier's perspective for twenty five years, and then owning apartments for a decade, Delbert McDougal felt he understood the real estate and housing industry well enough to start his own business.

Plus, he and Carolyn had developed a passion for the industry. Delbert focused on acquiring and financing the properties, while Carolyn managed and rented them, with maintenance help from their sons Marc and Mike.

LEAVING GE

In 1982, Delbert was ready to finally strike out on his own. He sat down with Carolyn and the boys to let them know what his plans were. They all knew that was what he'd been working toward, but there were concerns.

"I was identified as the 'GE man' in Lubbock. I never thought that my leaving the company would bother the boys, but they were nervous about it."

"After I graduated from high school," Marc said, "I moved to Artesia, New Mexico and worked in the oil field. At that time, I was sure that anything would be better than working for Delbert.

"When Delbert left GE, Mike was still in high school. I do think he was worried where our next meal would come from."

Carolyn was very happy with their life with GE and was the most afraid of the career move.

"My father worked for one company all his life, Carolyn said. "I was very concerned about leaving that monthly paycheck for the unknowns of owning our own business.

"I sought out Mary Tidwell, a close friend to share my fears. After listening to me for a few minutes, she said that when men get to be Delbert's age, they either change jobs or change wives.

"I said that it looks like I've made the cut. We both had a good laugh, and that helped me through my fears."

Delbert was surprised by his family's concern. But he was used to working around hurdles. But he also discussed his family's concerns with his pastor, Dr. Fred Meeks.

Crescent Apartments.

Following pages: Photos of apartments acquired through the 1980s.

Above: Country Village, a North Overton property.

Below: Waterford Place.

"We talked it through and prayed about it," Delbert said. "He encouraged me to go with my heart. He said that I should continue to pray about it, and if I felt confident about my ability to succeed, he believed my family would come around. It was right after that meeting with my pastor that I finally made the decision to leave GE."

Vin Sweeney helped Delbert grow with GE, and didn't want him to leave the company. But he was also a friend and when he could see that Delbert had made up his mind, he gave McDougal his blessing and encouragement

"Vin was one of my closest friends," Delbert said. "He had an important influence on my growth as a businessman."

Vin Sweeney retired and lived on the South Carolina coast until he passed away in 2006. He and Delbert spoke regularly by phone and saw each other from time to time. Vin's son John came to work in the McDougal's construction division in 1989, where he is today.

In 1982, after twenty-five years with the company Delbert notified his supervisor at GE that he was leaving the company. At that time, he was earning about $55,000 a year in salary and bonuses, plus a company car and benefits.

"The GE family was good to me and that's why I stayed so long," Delbert said.

"It was not an easy decision to leave after having worked there for twenty five years. But once I made the decision, I never looked back. I never considered the possibility I would fail."

"Failure was not an option."

A FAMILY BUSINESS

While Delbert handled the acquisition, financing, and oversaw maintenance, Carolyn managed the properties and leased them.

She worked in Overton almost every day, and saw first hand the steady deterioration of the neighborhood.

"Although crime was on the rise in this neighborhood," Carolyn said, "I was never afraid during our early years. But Delbert did begin to worry."

If Carolyn observed residents causing problems or not taking care of their apartment, she would confront them. More often than not, they would change their behavior. If not, she'd force them to vacate.

"These were less violent times," Carolyn said. "I was never afraid, and never backed down.

"One of my many friendships was with a man living in one of our North Overton units. I told him about evicting some people who lived down the hall from him. He said if anyone ever gave me any trouble to tell him and he'd 'take care of them.'

"I don't know what he meant by 'taking care of them' and never asked him for help. I always tried to earn the respect and friendship of our good renters.

"Like many of our renters in those early days, I still see this man from time to time and consider him a friend."

As the area deteriorated, Delbert became more concerned about Carolyn's safety. He

stayed in touch with her by phone several times a day.

As they had a number of apartments in a relatively close area, Carolyn would often just walk from one to the other.

"I often walked down the alleys to and from our properties," Carolyn said, "in order to visit with utilities workers about problems I needed repaired.

"As the years progressed, the workers advised me to stay out of the alleys, for my own safety."

But since her son Marc was helping her manage apartments, he was usually in the same area most of the day. One day he couldn't find Carolyn. For some reason, she was away from her office longer than he thought she should've been.

Marc grew more nervous as he went to each of their properties and couldn't find her. He called his Dad, who didn't know where she was, either. As it turned out, Marc had just missed Carolyn, as they were both traveling between apartments. The next day, Delbert handed Carolyn her first mobile phone.

"Cell phones had only recently been introduced," Carolyn noted.

"Mine was large and didn't work very well. But it did provide an extra layer of safety and more piece of mind for all of us."

On a few occasions the McDougals would take on the management of properties they didn't own. There was one particular property on Fifth street in North Overton they agreed to manage, and Carolyn walked through each unit to see what maintenance was needed.

She approached a young couple in another complex to see if they'd like to become resident managers in the Fifth Street property.

"They told me they would love to do that," Carolyn said. "They were very excited and began moving their furniture over to their new apartment. When they brought their second load over, the first load had already been stolen."

This was just the first of many crime problems at this complex. It didn't take long for Carolyn to see that there were more problems than she would be able to handle in this property.

"After a couple of days, I walked in to Delbert's office and put the apartment keys on his desk," Carolyn said.

"I told him that I would not go back to that property, and that I would not ask any of our employees to go back there either. It was just too dangerous. Delbert and I never asked any of our employees to do something we wouldn't do.

"Delbert terminated our management deal with the owner, and we moved the young couple back to a safer property."

Top, left: Cross Pointe.

Above: Gatewood.

Below: Sierra Crossing Apartments.

❖

Above: Marlboro Apartments, another North Overton property.

Below: Stratford Place.

While Carolyn managed the apartments, Marc and Mike would do maintenance chores in the evenings and on Saturdays. They all got to know their renters.

"We'd clean the apartments when they were vacant, and do yard and pool maintenance throughout the week," said Marc. "Carolyn befriended many of our earlier renters, which made it tough when they got behind on their rent. Delbert and Carolyn would work with anybody, if the renters would just be honest with them.

"We also learned a lot about human behavior from working in and around apartments. One of our renters had a bad drinking problem. I would have to go regularly to his apartment to let him in. He'd get so drunk he couldn't find his key."

WORKING TEENAGERS

"Growing up, we learned not to question Delbert's authority," said Marc. "If he grounded me for a week and I complained about it, he would automatically make it two weeks. I had a smart mouth, and had to re-learn that lesson a few times."

While Marc had a knack for pushing his dad's limits, Mike had the benefit of learning from his older brother's mistakes. But not always.

"I once tried to kill Marc with a fireplace poker. I was a senior in high school, and Marc had graduated but was living at home. We each had a beanbag chair in our bedrooms. One day after school, I was in my room doing homework and Marc and his future wife Pam were watching television in the den.

"They wanted to sit on the bean bag chairs, so Marc walked into my room and picked mine up without saying anything.

"I asked him what he was doing, and he said he was taking my chair. I told him he wasn't, but by that time, he was out the door with it. I followed him into the den, and told him to put my chair back in my room.

"He didn't even bother to acknowledge that I'd said anything. That really infuriated me.

"I grabbed the fireplace poker and threw it at him.

"It hit his raised arm and bounced on the floor.

"We had just moved into our new house and Marc and I both stopped in horror to see dark spots from the poker on Mom's new carpet.

"We were both in mortal danger at that point, so we forgot our argument about the beanbag chair.

"Mom would hold us equally responsible for ruining her new carpet, so we worked like mad to get the stains cleaned up before she got home.

"Luckily, the stains came out, and we were spared. I guess the Good Lord saved both our lives that day."

Delbert worked a lot, but he always made time for family. He and Carolyn were always at the important school, church, and sports events the boys participated in.

"Our two sons were very competitive growing up and often fought with each other, as boys tend to do," Carolyn said.

"But they never got in serious trouble. I'd always make them come kiss me goodnight when they got home. No matter how late their curfew was. I knew that would be a deterrent to drinking.

"One night, Delbert got a call from someone he knew saying that Marc had been disrespectful to him.

"As the story went, some boys threw something at a car that Marc and his friends were in. They stopped the car to confront the boys.

"A man was outside and saw what was happening, and came over to keep a fight from getting started. He sent Marc and his friends on their way, and evidently Marc said something ugly to him.

"We got in the car and found Marc and his friends. When we got home and we sat him down to discuss it, Marc didn't deny the man's account, but he said it was none of the man's business. Marc complained that the man should've stayed out of it.

"Delbert and I told Marc that he was never to be disrespectful to adults. We explained that if something needed to be said to an adult, Marc should come home and tell us, and we'll take care of it. We made Marc call the man and apologize.

On another occasion months later, Mike and a couple of his friends pelted a girl's car with raw eggs. The girl's mother saw them doing it, and called to tell Delbert what had happened.

Delbert told her Mike would be back over at their house the next morning to wash the car. And then he sat up and waited for Mike to come home.

"When I came home late that Saturday night," Mike remembers, "Delbert was standing at the front door glaring at me. To this day, I've never seen a more terrifying sight than dad waiting for me at the front door in his underwear."

The McDougals were well known, so neither boy had much of a chance of getting away with much in a town the size of Lubbock.

Meanwhile, the apartment complexes still weren't generating much cash flow. They were paying the mortgage and expenses, but Carolyn was not drawing a salary. They were building equity.

Most of the apartments were only full 9 months out of the year. What little they made, was put back into the apartments for repairs.

When it was time to replace their car, Delbert and Carolyn decided to splurge a little and reward themselves. They bought a used Cadillac.

"I can remember how excited I was about that Cadillac," Carolyn said. "I was so proud of it. We had worked hard and it was so much nicer than anything we'd ever driven. It felt so luxurious.

"Not long after we bought it, I had a fender-bender on the way to work. I was so upset.

Above: Inn Turn Apartments.

Below: Marc McDougal (left) with business associates in front of Hunter's Way, c. 1990.

"When Delbert called me at the office that morning, he could tell by my voice that something was wrong. I just couldn't bring myself to tell him what had happened.

"He kept pushing me to tell him what was wrong, and I finally started crying and said I had wrecked the car.

"He asked me if I was bleeding. I said no, I wasn't hurt.

"Then he said, 'Hush up crying. You're not hurt, and we can fix the car!'"

"I was so afraid he'd be mad at me, but he didn't ever say another word about it. He was very understanding."

THE FIRST EMPLOYEE

A few months after he started his business, Delbert invited Sylvia Vanstory to join him in his new company. Sylvia worked in the GE office, and she and Delbert had a mutual respect for each other. She said yes.

Soon after she joined Delbert, the rental housing and construction industries took a nose dive. Apartment units had been overbuilt and interest rates skyrocketed. People were bailing out of real estate in droves, but not Delbert McDougal.

"Delbert never gets discouraged, nor gives up," Sylvia said. "He is like the 'Energizer Bunny,' he just keeps on going."

Above: Cedar Ridge.

Below: University Square built by Delbert in Levelland, Texas in the early 1980s.

"He had to quit building apartments for awhile, but he was managing quite a few at that time. It was not an easy time. It was a struggle. Money was not plentiful, but he always found a way to make it work.

"I learned so many things from him during the lean years. He never stayed awake at night worrying about what to do next. He never became discouraged. His temperament is always the same. He's a problem solver."

THE EARLY APARTMENT FINANCIAL MODEL

After a few years in the business, Delbert had learned the finances of owning and running successful rental properties.

He knew how much each unit should cost, based on the rental income the market would allow. He also knew how to control maintenance costs, and Carolyn's people skills made her a great success at leasing and keeping the good tenants happy, and getting rid of the bad ones.

In the early years of his business, McDougal purchased older, small apartment complexes, with 15 to 25 individual one-bedroom units in each that needed work.

He'd have to pay about $7,500 per unit for a typical complex. In the case of a 16-unit property,

University Square, Levelland.

he'd pay in the neighborhood of $120,000, and would try to finance between 90 to 95 percent of the loan. That meant he'd have to come up with $10,000 to $12,000 for a down payment.

Interest rates were 10 percent at the time, so on a $110,000 note, he would have to pay $21,600 per year in principal, interest, taxes, and insurance.

Each apartment unit rented for $200 per month, and depending on vacancy rates, a sixteen unit property would generate from $35,000 to $38,000 per year.

Any cash flow would be used for utilities, maintenance, repair, administrative costs, and when any was left over, down payments on other properties.

Delbert realized how wasteful his renters were with their electricity use, since he paid their electric bills. He began installing individual electric meters, which made them more responsible with electricity use.

Individual electric meters are now required by state law, but Delbert was the first apartment owner in Lubbock to install them on his properties.

During this time, Delbert also gained strong experience in the financial side of the business. In the early years, he had to struggle to get adequate financing, but his good payment record made finding money easier each year.

Delbert knew that if he could expand his borrowing power, he could accelerate his profits. He found that opportunity in a partnership that had a cutting-edge apartment idea called modules.

BRINKCRAFT

Shortly after leaving GE, McDougal formed a partnership with Brinkcraft, Inc. to build modular apartments. Brinkcraft was a wholly owned subsidiary of the L. D. Brinkman Corporation, one of the world's largest carpet and flooring companies, based out of Kerrville, Texas.

"I saw an opportunity with the L. D. Brinkman group to build a large number of apartments with a piece of the ownership," Delbert said. "Brinkcraft had the financing capability to allow me to build a company at an accelerated rate."

The company built modular housing from a plant in Childress, about ninety miles from Lubbock. McDougal and L. D. Brinkman formed a joint venture that involved several corporate layers.

The L. D. Brinkman Corporation owned Brinkcraft, Inc., which was the manufacturer of the housing units. Brinkcraft then sold the apartment units to a separate corporation named Brinkcraft Development Company.

Delbert was the General Partner of the development company, but was not a partner in the other entities. That legal structure would benefit him in the coming years.

"My job was to find the locations, purchase the land, find the interim money to build the apartments, and oversee their construction,' he said.

"We were probably a little ahead of our time. It looked like you were stacking trailer houses on top of each other when they were being built. But if you looked at them when they were finished, it was nearly impossible to tell any difference between modular apartments and others built from the ground up."

The key advantage of modular construction was the absence of common walls between the apartments. Between each apartment was four inches of dead air space, which made them much quieter. It also provided better fire protection.

Delbert believed this type of construction was going to revolutionize the apartment industry. He built about twenty-five hundred total units for Brinkcraft.

But like the Las Colinas partnership, there was trouble ahead for Delbert in this partnership, too.

THE SAVINGS & LOAN COLLAPSE

In the late 1980s, there was a massive change in America's ownership of multi-family housing. Tax law changes took away popular tax shelters for rental property. Investors started unloading apartments at bargain prices.

This, along with a downturn in the market caused the financial collapse of many Savings & Loans, due to the large number of real estate loans made on properties with inflated values.

What was a crisis to owners and S&L's was an opportunity for McDougal, if he could secure financing.

Because of the plummeting housing values and resulting loan defaults, it was virtually impossible to borrow money for real estate purposes from the banks during this time.

Delbert believed that the problems in the housing industry in the 1980s were due to investors taking major risks, in order to avoid paying taxes to the IRS.

"These decisions were often made with the advice of their lawyers and accountants," Delbert noted, "who were making money by

Cedar Ridge.

Boardwalk Apartments.

creating and managing these investment partnerships. They were convenient tax shelters, but not sound real estate deals.

"Those tax shelters, coupled with an overabundance of bad real estate loans by the Savings and Loan industry, resulted in unsecured paper profits based on over-appraised properties.

"The S&Ls made loans to unsophisticated buyers with no knowledge of the real value of housing."

When the market collapsed, the country was left with a devastated housing market. But it also created an opportunity for someone with experience in the industry.

With a shrewd understanding of the market, property with artificially high values could now be purchased at prices well below market value.

Delbert's challenge was to acquire funds to purchase properties at a cost that would allow him to pay high interest rates, and still cash flow the properties.

"My philosophy was to exercise from a position of strength, when in fact my cash position was extremely weak," Delbert explained. "I would offer letters of intent and continue to negotiate pricing based on low interest rates while scrambling to come up with closing funds."

Delbert had borrowed money from a number of individuals around the country over the years, and his excellent payment history allowed him to go back to them for additional money. McDougal found financiers locally, as well as syndication groups from around the country.

In order to make the most of this strategy, it was necessary for Delbert to negotiate hard, and exercise extreme patience. It sometimes took up to two years to finalize a sale. This could only be accomplished during a time when there were few buyers at the table.

After a few successful closings, word got out and financial institutions with notes on housing properties began calling Delbert.

VISION FOR MCDOUGAL PROPERTIES

As his purchases increased in the 1980s, Delbert began to look at what he was paying to real estate agents and construction crews.

In his long-term corporate vision, he knew he could save money, and create new profit centers by acquiring his own real estate agency and construction company. It was in the aftermath of the S&L housing crisis that McDougal's corporate vision reached a tipping point.

He purchased two small real estate companies in 1988, and began saving 2 to 3 percent of the purchase price of apartments he was acquiring at fire sale prices. That resulted in ongoing operating capital for the benefit of the newly formed McDougal Properties, the apartment management arm of the business.

The success in acquiring a growing number of older apartment units created a need for an in-house construction company to perform renovations. By doing so, Delbert was able to insure he could perform renovations at cost, and at the same time, take on outside projects that would bring additional profits to his growing business.

After short stints in the oil fields and an auto parts store, McDougal's older son Marc moved back home.

"I came back home to save some money, and went to work managing and doing maintenance at the Garden Court Apartments in North Overton, near the Texas Tech campus" Marc said.

"Delbert wanted to get into the construction business, so after a short while he moved me out of apartments and I started building homes. During high school, I did summer work in the construction industry for another local builder. I learned how to do plumbing, sheet rocking, and a little roofing."

"In addition to using Marc for construction," Delbert explained, I hired David Miller to come on staff with me and begin his long career with us.

Miller had been working with Delbert at Brinkcraft. David worked in the plant that built the modular apartments in Childress, Texas. As the relationship between Delbert and Brinkcraft deteriorated, David was sent to Lubbock to keep tabs on what Delbert was doing.

"When Delbert offered me a job," David said, "I didn't hesitate. I knew what kind of man he was, and I knew I wanted to align my future with him."

"I wanted to move Marc over to the home building and realtor division, so I wanted someone with David's experience to create a full-time construction company for us," Delbert said.

David Miller, president of McDougal Construction.
PHOTO BY CHILDRESS PHOTOGRAPHY.

Miller's expertise and contacts helped him grow the construction division, and allowed the company to maintain a steady construction crew for apartment rehabs.

Like many of Delbert's early hires, David Miller is still with the company.

Miller's entry into the construction business also allowed Marc to create a home building unit as an additional profit center. Building speculative and custom houses made sure they always had work for their construction crews, and didn't have to continually hire and lay off workers with the ups and downs of the apartment occupancies.

"I felt that if our single-family construction unit was going to survive, we needed to form our own development opportunities," Delbert said. "This comes from my desire to control my own destiny in deals, from start to finish."

Delbert began to see opportunities to purchase land for future development, which required him to hold properties as long as seven years.

McDougal also began managing apartment complexes they didn't own. Property management gave the growing company a fifth profit center.

The circle of companies McDougal envisioned was now a reality. He had a growing

❖

Top: University Park, Levelland.

Middle: Windy Ridge.

Bottom: Twin Oaks Apartments.

market share of apartments, a realty company, a construction division, a development company, and a property management company.

McDougal had seen an opportunity to expand his business during a severe downturn in the housing industry. He was now well positioned to take advantage of the coming upturn.

Like most entrepreneurs, Delbert kept a hand in every aspect of the business. He paid the bills, and handled the ever-present problem of collecting past-due rents.

THE COAT

While he's known for his hard driving personality and bulldog determination to succeed, Delbert felt like his renters were a part of the family.

Carolyn tells a story that has become part of McDougal company lore.

"Back in the early years of our business, we were barely making enough money to pay all the bills," Carolyn remembered. "What little we made went back into the apartments for repairs.

"We had a young man in our Country Village Apartments who had not paid his rent. He was a college student, and told us he had spoken to his mother, who would send us a check by the end of the week. When the check didn't arrive as promised, I called his mother. She had no idea that her son owed rent, but told me that he would have to take care of his own bills.

"I mentioned this to Delbert after he got home that evening. The next morning was a cold and rainy Saturday morning, and Delbert left the house early to confront the young man. This is one of the hardest parts about the apartment business.

"When Delbert would make these visits to renters who were past due, he would either get some money, a firm commitment when he would have the rent in hand, or tell them to move out, based on his trust in what they had to say.

"About an hour later, Delbert returned home without his coat. It seems he had found the renter walking in the parking lot outside his apartment."

"The student was on his way to the local convenience store with no coat, to buy something to eat with the few dollars he had in his pocket."

"After discussing the situation with the young man, Delbert gave him some more time to get his rent paid. Then, he gave the boy his coat."

"He left the house as an angry apartment manager, but returned a concerned father."

"That is the Delbert not everyone sees."

The Boardwalk Apartments.

CHAPTER 4

HARD BUSINESS LESSONS, 1984-1990

Soon after Delbert McDougal left GE in 1982, he became involved in a complex business partnership with L. D. Brinkman, who owned several businesses related to the housing industry.

As General Manager for Brinkcraft Development Company, Delbert's job was to find the locations for apartment complexes, purchase the land, secure an interim loan to build the apartments, and oversee their construction.

This business arrangement worked successfully for several years. But by the mid-1980s, Delbert began to notice that his profits from this venture were shrinking.

"I acquired the land, found the loans, got the property ready to build, bought the modules from Brinkman, and then operated the property under West Texas Management," Delbert remembered.

"Every time I thought I had made a good profit on an apartment complex, I'd get another invoice from the factory, saying that prices had gone up. I thought they were getting greedy."

"I should have had some control over their prices, but I didn't. They just kept sending invoices after the fact."

Adding to the rising costs, the IRS changed the tax laws, which closed most tax shelters for investors in apartments. At that point, there was little advantage for absentee owners participating in apartment projects. Apartment building pretty much stopped, except in fast-growth cities.

Delbert began to suspect that Brinkman was liquidating. The Development Company was not a part of the L. D. Brinkman Corporation. It was a stand alone company.

"I believed that in order to make sure I remained with all the debt, Brinkman kept the Development Company separate from their umbrella company," Delbert said.

As he feared, in 1986 Brinkcraft filed Chapter 7 bankruptcy. This left Delbert as the managing partner of the development company.

Sagewood, a modular complex built by Brinkcraft.

Above: Sandlewood, another Brinkcraft property.

Below: The Quadrangle, later named The Colonies.

"I believe they thought they could run me off. But I was the general partner, so I still controlled all the properties."

"I informed them of that fact. They didn't believe it, but I told them to read the contract."

"I was liable for more than $5 million of debt, held some notes on property we'd sold, and controlled the management and cash we produced.

"It was certainly not a very good position to be in, but it was the best option I could see and was determined not to lose what I had. I got a harsh lesson on dealing with large corporations and how they could use their power to run over individuals.

"Because of the method in which all monies from loans were handled and transferred directly into L. D. Brinkman's corporate account, I believed I could prove in court that the actual funds from the Development Company were taken into the L. D. Brinkman Corporation.

"If I prevailed, then Mr. Brinkman would become the responsible party, and I would be relieved from the guarantees."

McDougal contacted the lender, First Gibraltor Savings in California. Brinkcraft owed Gibraltor $5 million. They were most interested in talking to Delbert. He helped Gibraltor's auditors and attorneys sort through all the Brinkman companies and their relationships.

When Gibraltor figured out what was going on, they asked McDougal to testify against the partnership during the trial, which took place in San Antonio.

His testimony was crucial to Gibraltor's winning the court case.

McDougal also showed Gibraltor how he could keep the properties solvent, and pledged to help the bank get their money back.

University Arms.

"Fortunately," Delbert said, "the lender believed that I was honest and capable of pulling it off."

Delbert was able to maintain his ownership of the properties. Of course that meant he also had a huge liability to manage.

He subsequently worked out an agreement with the outside financial syndicates who had also invested in the project. Delbert personally guaranteed all debt and operating costs on all their properties for a period of two years from the purchase date.

"Most of these relationships were forged during a difficult time," Delbert remembered. "But many of these same lenders have done business with me again and again.

"I didn't want my credibility or their money to be lost by fraud or mismanagement."

McDougal turned a potential disaster into a positive for his new company by knowing what was possible, and not taking the easy out.

"If this deal had crumbled, it would have devastated me financially and killed my dream of building my company," Delbert now admits.

"Carolyn was afraid of getting involved in the extensive legal battles to get the property. But I felt it was the right thing to do."

"My nightmares from the Las Colinas problems came back," Carolyn remembered. "This lawsuit scared me to death.

"I am not a risk taker. But by then I had a lot of confidence in Delbert. His instincts are very good, and he's proven to be right most of the time."

In the long run, Delbert came out a winner. McDougal wound up owning a lot of new properties, his most important goal. He also survived another sharp business lesson.

But he also shouldered a significant amount of debt. He had very little cash and was not out of danger. Delbert restructured his debt, and pressed on. Before long, he was able to continue buying properties on the still-depressed market.

Some people believe that problems come in threes. In Delbert's case, that would prove to be true. He soon found himself in the middle of another financial crisis.

THE QUADRANGLE SURPRISE

"Brinkcraft was using funds from two investment packagers," Delbert explained. "The syndicators would round up investors from the East Coast who were looking for tax breaks and higher returns on their money."

These were not large investors, but typically doctors and other professionals who were looking to improve on what they could get out of a savings or money market account. Instead of tax breaks, Delbert's partnership was paying the investors high interest rates for the use of their money. They had no ownership in the apartments.

Delbert had met several of the syndicators in person, and began using them for financing in some projects after severing his relationship with Brinkcraft.

"In our business relationship," said Delbert, "I agreed to be a 50/50 partner. The syndicator would raise the money, and I would buy, renovate, and manage the properties. We'd split the profits equally."

One project in Lubbock with syndicator-provided financing was called The Quadrangle.

He raised more than $400,000 for this apartment project. That money was supposed to come to Delbert to buy the property, renovate it, and get it back on the market.

In the midst of the project, Delbert started getting calls from investors looking for their payments on the investment.

"I told them I wasn't aware they were a part of the project, Delbert remembered. "After providing some documentation, I believed the syndicator had pocketed some of the money he was supposed to send me."

"I confronted him about the missing money and offered him a deal.

"To avoid prosecution, he agreed to give up his fifty percent interest in the apartments. In exchange, I took over all the apartments and all the debt.

McDougal paid every one of the investors what they were owed.

"I knew it was the right thing to do, because the syndicator had used my name to lure these folks into the project," Delbert said.

This was not an easy path to take. While it did provide him the opportunity to acquire more property, this project was not cash flowing at this time. It took Delbert several years to get all his investors paid in full, but he got it done.

McDougal learned another key lesson about knowing who he was doing business with.

Every investor who was involved in these projects was paid back with interest. Some of the investors in this project approached McDougal about financing more of his projects. They appreciated the commitment Delbert made to make sure they had come out whole.

"I was gratified by their confidence, and have used them as financial resources periodically through the years. Twenty plus years later, I've still never met many of them face-to-face."

Each of these situations soured McDougal on partnerships, a distaste he retains to this day. In each case, he could've been financially ruined. However, Delbert found a way to turn potential disasters in to positives.

With determination, McDougal acquired a significant amount of rental property in a short amount of time. He was becoming a major housing player in the Lubbock market.

THE CHAUFFEUR

Like their young business, the McDougal marriage had its tests. One warm Saturday afternoon, Delbert dropped Carolyn off at the grocery store while he went to fill the car with gas.

After arriving back home, Delbert stopped in the den to see what the boys were watching on television. A while later, he asked the boys where

An example of an older property in North Overton.

their mother was. Without bothering to look up from the television, they shrugged their shoulders.

Shortly thereafter, Carolyn appeared at the front door with both arms full of groceries and a less than happy demeanor.

"Now, we go to the grocery store together," Carolyn laughs as she recalls the legendary family story.

"People often make fun of how much time Delbert and I spend together. I just tell them I don't want Delbert to drive off and forget me again."

A BANKING LESSON

Another property that McDougal acquired during this period was Cedar Ridge Apartments. The property was losing money, so to avoid foreclosure, the owner made an agreement with his bank to deed the property to McDougal. Delbert knew the property was well located for Lubbock's future growth, and with strong management, would eventually make money.

So he acquired the property from the bank by assuming the debt and negative cash flow. The bank was delighted to unload the apartment complex.

Banks had been burned in the great real estate collapse in the '80s, and now they were keeping a tight rein on their holdings. A year later, the bank's auditor contacted Delbert with concerns about the note.

Above: University Arms, now demolished.

Below: Cross Point Apartments.

Substandard residential homes in North Overton.

After selling the property to McDougal, the bank had evidently booked this loan as a loss in their portfolio, even though Delbert had not missed a payment.

"The apartment wasn't making money when I took over the note," said Delbert. "It was aggravating that they would sell me the property, then complain about the deal they'd made a year later. They wanted me to pay off more of the note, which I wouldn't do."

In time, the bank moved on to other matters, and Cedar Ridge began cash flowing. Now, it's one of the most profitable properties in McDougal's rental portfolio.

These were difficult years for McDougal's young company. He knew that he could've been put out of business several times, and that he had a number of problems to work out. He saw others give up and take jobs with other companies.

Reflecting on these difficulties Delbert said, "I've observed over the years that when people are confronted with a problem in their business that will require some rethinking, or hard work, or even going to court, more and more they throw their hands up and file bankruptcy.

"As a society, I believe we are too willing to take the easy way out, and let the public pick up the tab. This does not make good business people or leaders."

ON RELATIONSHIPS WITH LENDERS

By this time, McDougal understood that a good relationship with his bankers meant that they needed to understand his business. And just as importantly, they needed to have confidence in him.

"They've got to believe you can do what you say," Delbert said.

"When you take a proposal to a banker, you have to remember they've seen thousands of them. There has never been a bad deal made on a piece of paper.

"Bankers are not developers, apartment owners, or builders. They can't run your business for you. But the best bankers are those who are good sounding boards for you. They can ask tough questions, help you work through issues, and share the experiences from other businesses they've worked with."

Most importantly, Delbert knew that when his bankers made money, they'll be easier to sell on the next project.

Delbert's history of working through problems told bankers and private investors that they could depend on him.

NORTH OVERTON IN DECLINE

While Delbert was fighting to save his business from the partnership threats, his initial investments were also being threatened by the deterioration of the North Overton neighborhood.

This neighborhood, between Texas Tech and downtown Lubbock, was clearly in distress. Absentee owners didn't manage their properties, which in turn brought about their rapid decline.

Now, the once proud neighborhood was plagued with falling rents and property values. Crime soared.

The demise of North Overton was further hastened by the sellout of the apartments to out-of-state syndicates. During this time, Lubbock began building Interstate 27, which displaced a number of low income renters. Many were relocated to North Overton.

A number of out-of-town owners of apartments in Overton were among those who agreed to house those displaced by the freeway demolition.

Delbert learned that some of these apartment syndicates were paid up to four years of rent in advance by the state, by agreeing to house these displaced renters.

"Looking back, it was apparent to me that these syndicates took the money and virtually left their

More North Overton homes awaiting demolition.

Chapter 4 ✦ 39

North Overton properties awaiting demolition.

apartments unsupervised," Delbert said. "That was the final straw in the demise of the area."

Delbert and other concerned property owners began to attend meetings called by City leaders to discuss what could be done to turn the neighborhood problem around.

In 1986, the "Overton Revitalization Plan" was released. It was the joint project headed by the Institute for Urban Studies International at Texas Tech University, prepared with input from the Lubbock Redevelopment Association, Overton Neighborhood Association, and the City of Lubbock Planning and Zoning Commission and staff.

The study reported the following objectives:
- To reduce the crime rate in the Overton Addition.
- To encourage efforts to rehabilitate the real estate in the area.
- To be a catalyst for the many segments of the community, such as the City Council, Lubbock Independent School District, Texas Tech University, business and professional people, and homeowners, to make the Overton area a beautiful and inviting place to live, to do business and to raise families.

In the foreword to the study, W. R. Collier, president of the Lubbock Redevelopment Association, wrote:

The plan that has been developed by this study is a far-sighted, long-range plan that will take patience and understanding by all parties involved. The challenges, opportunities and pursuit of excellence are in our hands as citizens of the City of Lubbock. As the plan is implemented and goals are accomplished, the citizens of Lubbock will benefit greatly from this revitalization effort.

W. R. Collier is also the president of American State Bank, one of Lubbock's leading banks, whose main branch sat across the street from Overton. No one knew better the impact of Overton's decline than Mr. Collier.

After the report was released, another round of meetings ensued between the City Council,

Above: A North Overton property awaiting demolition.

Below: Fourplex in North Overton.

Chapter 4 ◆ 41

◆

North Overton apartments awaiting demolition.

the business community, various redevelopment interests, and private developers.

South Overton residents organized a neighborhood association and began some initiatives to instill pride of ownership.

But in North Overton, there was no momentum to effectively reverse its decline. There were too many absentee owners, and too much crime.

The Revitalization Plan, correctly analyzed the problems, and suggested some remedies. But it sat on desks all around Lubbock while the neighborhood decay continued to spread.

"The more of these meetings I went to, the more convinced I was that nothing was going to get done," Delbert said.

The problems seemed too complex. While there were several blocks with well-kept homes, acquiring enough property to effectively start removing the blighted areas was widely viewed as a legal and financial quagmire. Delbert was also convinced that Lubbock taxpayers would never let the city government do an urban redevelopment project on this scale.

North Overton was not presenting the kind of image that Texas Tech, nor the downtown business community, could afford to have adjacent to them. But no one seemed to have vision to tackle the problem.

The neighborhood was in a tailspin.

CHAPTER 5

Changes in the Marketplace, 1990-1999

By 1990, the majority of Delbert McDougal's properties were scattered throughout south and west Lubbock, with some long-term properties acquired for future development to the west and north.

While he never planned to give up his oldest properties in central Lubbock, the growing blight in the area forced him to begin selling them off.

By this time, Delbert, Carolyn, and Marc had grown the business into a multimillion dollar company.

Delbert kept a strong hand in all of the Company's ventures, but focused on acquiring new properties, and securing financing.

Carolyn continued to train staff and work in the apartment offices, oversee government housing regulations, and handle the decorating decisions. Marc focused on new home construction, apartment maintenance, and managing the realty.

Even with the growth of their business, Delbert and Carolyn still had regular contact with their renters.

"We had two young men renting from us who worked for a seismograph company," Carolyn said. "We learned they were laid off from their job, and soon thereafter, their car broke down. After a few weeks, I got concerned they were running out of money.

"We knew they were good kids that had run into hard times, so I went to the grocery store and bought a few staples for them. Delbert went with me to deliver the groceries, and gave them some cash on the way out of the apartment.

For many years, the Lubbock Lions Club has held an all day pancake breakfast in the fall to raise money for the charities they supported.

Delbert and Carolyn would buy dozens of extra tickets to this event, and would give them to any renters they knew were struggling to make ends meet.

Ashton Pointe Apartments, built in 1996.

PHOTOS BY CHILDRESS PHOTOGRAPHY.

"We tried to be understanding landlords," Carolyn said. We couldn't help feeling a little parental responsibility to the young folks who rented from us."

In 1984, the McDougal's younger son Mike graduated from high school and moved to Fort Worth to attend Texas Christian University.

After earning his degree in Accounting and acquiring his CPA license, Mike joined Ernst & Young's Ft. Worth office in 1988.

ANOTHER PRODIGAL SON RETURNS

Four years later, Mike called Delbert to say one of Ernst & Young's clients had offered him a large salary to open their new Nashville headquarters.

With all of McDougal Companies' growth, Delbert had been contemplating asking Mike to return to the family business. He knew he could use someone with strong financial experience. Someone he could trust.

"When Mike called me about his opportunity to move to Nashville, he was very excited, but wanted to discuss his options." Delbert remembers.

"I told him to forget going to Nashville, that I needed a financial officer and would pay him more to join the family business."

"He said that I didn't know how much they'd offered him. I told him it didn't matter."

It was an offer Mike couldn't refuse. He was in Lubbock three weeks later.

When Mike left for college in 1984, McDougal Properties owned fewer than one thousand apartment units and had just a few employees. During the eight years he was gone, the company more than doubled. He had a lot of catching up to do.

"When I returned," Mike said, "Delbert had doubled the size of the company. But he had continued to run it as he had from the beginning.

"Delbert would start negotiating for a property and then start looking for financing. He was constantly battling cash flow problems. He signed every check by hand. I don't know how he did it all.

"In my first meeting with our company's outside accountant, he told me only half-jokingly that Delbert had been bankrupt for years, but didn't know it. He was not exaggerating by much."

One of the first issues Mike had to deal with was the financial drain from the Quadrangle Apartments property, which Delbert took over after an out of town financier skimmed money from individual investors in the project.

The financial pressures on the company at that time were great, and McDougal could ill afford to be losing money in this deal. Interest rates were still high.

"Delbert believed that if he would spend his time making the project work, rather than paying lawyers and investing time in a lawsuit, he could salvage his relationships with these investors," Mike said.

The Dominion, luxury apartment community built in 2000.

 Inside the Dominion.

"I've never seen Delbert back out of a deal. He has faced down numerous problems but he never gives up."

Mike recognized that the company wasn't fully utilizing its equity to increase its borrowing power.

"Mike took the checkbook away from me and computerized our financial operations," Delbert said. He helped us grow our company."

During the 1990s, it was not unusual for McDougal to have more than $10 million in debt. As the cash flow situation improved, McDougal increased his acquisitions.

In 1993, Delbert asked Mike to begin quietly shopping his properties in the historic North Overton neighborhood, the area where he first began.

"We had more than 250 apartment units in North Overton, Mike said. "Our properties were losing value because of the declining values around us. "Over the next couple of years, I sold all but seventy units."

THE BIG DREAM

"In my first years back with the company, I was amazed at how Delbert could keep up with so much financial information in his head," Mike said. "He has an incredible mind for numbers.

"Even years after he turned the management of the apartments over to me, Delbert could still tell me within a few dollars how much each of our dozens of complexes were making in any given month."

Little did Mike know that Delbert was keeping something else in his head.

Jerry Roberson is an investment analyst for McDougal Properties. He had been with McDougal for more than ten years, when Delbert put him on a secret project.

"Delbert came in to my office one day in 1994," Jerry said. "From time to time we had talked about the various approaches to fixing the North Overton problem."

"I knew Delbert was selling his properties there. One day, he walked in and closed my office door and told me he wanted to do the research on who owned each parcel of land in North Overton. He wanted me to give him an idea of how much it would cost to buy every piece of property in the subdivision."

Roberson told McDougal it could take a couple of years to figure all that out, since North Overton was more than three hundred acres in size and totally developed. There were more than nine hundred separate parcels and structures there.

Delbert told him to get to work on it, and to keep it quiet.

RAISING THE COMPANY'S PROFILE

With all the properties McDougal accumulated, they were buying a fair amount of advertising. The realty company was located on the South Loop, which had turned into the highest traffic corridor in the city.

Mike McDougal, president, McDougal Properties.

Several years earlier, Marc changed the name of the realty division to McDougal Realtors. That name exposure brought additional value to all their enterprises.

In addition to their signage and advertising, the McDougal family began accepting high profile appointments to public boards in the community.

Delbert and Carolyn both felt strongly they should give back to their community, and had long been active volunteers at their church, and in their business associations.

The family also encouraged their employees to become active in community service, and allowed them to volunteer on company time.

The building and housing industry are highly regulated by cities and states, so it's natural for builders and developers to take an interest in government.

Delbert served as President of the West Texas Home Builders Association and the Lubbock Apartment Association, and in 1993 became President of the Texas Apartment Association. These positions gave him more contact with state and federal elected officials.

"Running for a public office requires a lot of time and sacrifice," Delbert said. "I believe we have an obligation to do what we can to insure the public's business is well managed, and to support those who get elected.

McDougal's sons followed their dad's footsteps in accepting leadership roles in their local, state, and national industry associations.

Marc became the first McDougal to hold a public office. In 1996, he was approached to run for the Lubbock County Republican Party chairmanship. He accepted, and won that race.

Two years later, Marc was elected to the City Council, and in 2002 became mayor of Lubbock, which he held for two terms before leaving office.

CHANGING APARTMENT FINANCIAL MODELS

The apartment business still formed the core of McDougal Properties' income, supplemented by the property management, construction, realtor's commissions, and development.

But the economics of apartment ownership had changed dramatically since Delbert and Carolyn bought that first sixteen-unit property in 1972.

In the early years of his business, McDougal purchased older, small apartment complexes, each with 15 to 25 individual one-bedroom units that needed work.

He'd have to pay about $6,500 per unit for a typical complex. He financed between 90 to 95 percent of the loan at 10 percent interest. He would pay about $21,000 per year in principal, interest, taxes, and insurance, and with normal occupancy, could bring in more than $35,000 per year, before maintenance costs.

In the late 1980s, McDougal began urchasing larger complexes. The typical property they bought during this time was more than twenty years old, had one hundred units, a high vacancy rate, and were often purchased out of foreclosure.

The cost per unit had risen to $10,000 in the ensuing decade, which meant a $1 million purchase price for a 100-unit property.

In this case, Delbert would usually put no money down and sign a personal note for the loan, which was generally in the ten percent interest range.

He would then raise $500,000 at 12 to 15 percent from investors to remodel the entire apartment. The rehab would take several months, using McDougal Construction to complete the work.

It would normally take McDougal Property Management twelve months to fully renovate and lease the apartments at $375 per unit.

Under the new business plan, the payments for principal, interest, taxes, insurance, and expenses on this project would be about $360,000 per year. After figuring in the lost revenue for the first year, the company would break even at just over eighty percent occupancy. Plus, they would produce income for the construction and management divisions for their work on the property.

As soon as possible, McDougal would pay off his investor note, and then go back to them when he found another property to renovate, This was a much more favorable business plan than in the early days. But it required a good knowledge of how much it would take to renovate a property, and the understanding of the market to know if they could be rented on a timely basis.

Delbert's instincts were good. In spite of the cyclical world of rental housing, he rarely misjudged a property or the state of the rental market.

Marc McDougal after he was elected mayor of Lubbock, 2002.

McDougal Realtors, 1986.

WORKING AS A FAMILY

Having four family members running a high stakes, fast-paced business can make for interesting relationships at the office. The McDougals have found a way to make it work.

"After Mike returned to the company, Delbert and I began to think about transition planning," Carolyn said.

Marc was building the real estate agency. Mike was more interested in the apartment business, which he took over from Delbert and Carolyn. Delbert was able to focus on the development side of the business.

There were plenty of disagreements between the two sons and their parents. Delbert tried to let those issues work themselves out, but would cast the deciding vote when necessary.

"Our family is very good at handling disagreement," Marc said. " We can go to the mat on specific issues, but always behind closed doors."

"But we also get over our anger right away. After a decision is made, we move on and all work together. We don't disagree publicly, and we respect each other's turf."

"Marc and I are complete opposites," Mike said. "He likes to hunt and play golf. I have no interest in outdoor sports. He's a salesman, I'm an accountant."

The sons have completely different responsibilities within the company, and each one respects the other's territory. If there are disagreements on overlapping issues that can't be resolved, Delbert makes the decisions.

"Usually the things we argue about are on the minor decisions," Delbert said. We have the same overall philosophy about how to run the company. We all have a desire to grow the business, so our employees can prosper with us.

"I'm very proud that my sons have been willing to come home and help me build this company," Delbert said. "I'm sure they thought twice before they were confident enough to come back and be a part of it.

One way the family relaxes is to escape to a small home Delbert bought on a nearby lake.

"Delbert likes to mow the grass at our lake house," said Mike McDougal. Delbert has a small Kaboda tractor, and the first thing he does is get on that tractor and mow our yard. Then he'll start mowing our neighbors' yards.

Delbert has a long time friend who lives next door, and when they're both at thelake, they'll try to see who can outmow the other. Delbert usually takes his pet schnauzer with him on the tractor while he's mowing. Sometimes he'll mow four or five yards. It's hilarious to watch."

THE DREAM TAKES SHAPE

After about a year of research, Jerry Roberson gave Delbert some promising news.

Jerry found it was possible to acquire a substantial enough piece of the North Overton properties on the west side of the project, with only a few purchases.

This was the side of the property adjacent to Texas Tech University, and where the most commercial value sat. If Roberson was correct, Delbert believed that one-third of the 325 acres could be acquired and allow him to fund the rest of the redevelopment project.

Delbert began to believe it would be possible to take on the whole project himself.

Carolyn wasn't pleased to hear him talk about it.

"Delbert talked about fixing North Overton for many years," Carolyn said. I was glad when the talk died down.

Though the years, most of the discussion had revolved around restoration. Delbert was looking at bulldozing the majority of North Overton and starting over.

"He was sixty-three years old when he started talking seriously about taking the project on himself," Carolyn said. "I really didn't want him to do that.

"We'd worked so hard and had achieved some success. I couldn't see taking on all those headaches and all that risk."

Less than two years after he began selling all their properties in North Overton, Delbert walked in to Mike's office and told him to stop selling them off. The dream had not died.

NORTH OVERTON STATISTICS

In 2000, there were about seventeen apartment units spread across the property in various stages of demise. According to the 2000 Census of Population and Housing, there were 4,725 residents in North Overton and 2,167 households. After McDougal started the process of contacting owners, he estimated the actual number living in the neighborhood during this time was twenty-five hundred.

While less than two percent of the city's population resided here, the area accounted for twenty-eight percent of the city's crime.

The oldest home in the area was built about 1908. There were more than 900 separate structures spread out over 325 acres. Incredibly, more than ninety-four percent of these structures were owned by people living outside of Lubbock.

Almost forty-seven percent of all Lubbock employees worked within two miles of North Overton during this time. In addition to Texas Tech and the downtown business and legal community, Lubbock's extensive medical community was located about two miles away.

Thirteen thousand people attended church within a mile of the project each week, and more than 25,000 students were enrolled at Texas Tech University, right next door.

"North Overton was right in the middle of all this business, educational, and religious activity," Jerry Roberson noted.

"It seemed to us that thousands of people could live here and walk to school, work, and church, if they chose to do so. That's what makes North Overton so valuable."

After gathering all the information they could about ownership, demographics, and property values, McDougal began to test the market.

When Delbert began to get some idea about what he'd have to pay for property in North Overton, he sent option contracts to all the vacant lot owners who didn't live in Lubbock.

"We sent it as an anonymous letter," Delbert said, "using a post office box return address. We got a surprisingly good response.

The very first response he received was from an owner who wrote that he would give McDougal his lot, if the transaction would be completed before December 31, about a month away.

"He was tired of paying taxes, and paying to keep it mowed," Marc said. "A couple of weeks

Delbert and "Lady" mowing at the lake home.

❖ *More North Overton homes.*

later, the deal was closed for the cost of attorney's fees."

Other deals followed, including several properties that were purchased for what was owed in taxes.

After a few months of responses and closings, Delbert believed he could acquire what was needed to capture the western portion of the 325-acre neighborhood.

If that was possible, he would be able to get his investment back with a little profit, and then slowly acquire and redevelop the remainder of North Overton.

Delbert had made the decision to move forward. He was going to do the project himself. Now, he had to convince his family partners.

"I remember that Delbert and I were sitting in Mike's office," Marc said. "Delbert told us that he wanted to pursue the North Overton project himself.

"He had been doing research and had a good handle on what it would take to buy the whole property. He saw how important the tract could be to Tech and downtown when it was totally redone to fit the needs of that area.

"After he left, I closed the door and told Mike that Delbert had lost his mind."

"Mike had already been running the numbers, and told me he believed Delbert might be on to something.

The family knew that Delbert had been researching the project, and had begun purchasing some of the commercial property. But they had not considered the idea of taking on the whole 325 acres.

"To do so would require our borrowing at least $30 million," Mike said. "What he was proposing was to risk everything we had all built on this one project. "

Delbert made his pitch to Carolyn, Marc, and Mike. They all knew how serious he was about it, and knew that when his mind was made up, it was virtually impossible to change it.

"After he discussed it with the boys, I asked them to help me talk Delbert out of going forward with the idea," Carolyn said. "I reminded them of Delbert's age, and the incredible stress this was going to put on him, and all of us.

North Overton propertues before demolition.

"I knew that this was an important project to Delbert, and to Lubbock. But I was afraid."

After Marc and Mike bought in to Delbert's vision, they both tried to help their mother feel better about it. It took some time, but eventually, Carolyn began to accept the idea.

"After I saw Marc and Mike get excited about the idea, I began to get more comfortable with it," Carolyn said.

"At our age, I was ready to slow down. Delbert accomplished many things in his career, but this was a mind boggling project. But I could see that Marc and Mike would be working side by side with Delbert, and I eventually decided that there was no way we could fail."

With everyone now on board, the McDougals planned their strategy. It is hard to keep a secret in a town Lubbock's size, and word was spreading that Delbert was buying property in North Overton.

"When it became apparent that we could acquire significant amounts of properties with relatively few transactions, we started buying," Mike said.

"We had to repurchase all the rental properties we had recently sold. In some cases, I was able to buy some properties back cheaper than what we'd sold them for two years earlier. In a few cases, we bought the same property three times."

Delbert was anxious to announce his plans. He decided that the time was right to let people know what he was planning.

"I knew that my announcement would start driving up prices," Delbert said, but I didn't want to conceal our plans any longer so I could move more quickly."

On Wednesday, July 21, 1999, with his family by his side, Delbert McDougal announced his plans to acquire and redevelop the historic North Overton area.

Initial reaction from the business community was mixed.

Business and city leaders were clearly elated, though they privately wondered how it would be possible for a local company to finance such an ambitious venture.

"A number of people told me I was crazy," Delbert said. "They said there was no way I could get this done."

McDougal knew that owners were going to hold out selling to drive the price of their property up. He'd heard everything that had been said about the problems in redeveloping North Overton for the previous fifteen years.

There were challenges ahead, with property owners spread all over the country. But Delbert had done his homework.

"I knew that I would be able to acquire enough of the commercial property fairly quickly to get that part done," Delbert said.

"The residential redevelopment would require more patience. I knew I could use profits from the commercial ventures and in time would get the rest of the project finished. I would work out the details as I went along."

THE BANKER'S DANCE

There is an old saying among bankers: Loan someone a million dollars and they'll dance for you. Loan someone ten million dollars, and you'll dance for them

One of Delbert McDougal's qualities is his quick sense of humor. When asked to introduce a prominent banker at a local charity function, he used that humor to illustrate the relationship between a borrower and his banker.

Alan White, CEO Of Plains Capital Bank was being honored. White had built Plains into the one of the largest banks in the region, and they

Alan White, CEO of Plains Capital Bank.

held notes on a significant number of McDougal's properties at the time.

Delbert began his introduction by running down the long list of White's accomplishments, which most in the room already knew.

McDougal wrapped up his introduction by saying, "But in spite of all of Alan White's success, he is just one phone call away from being the largest property owner in Lubbock."

The statement got the intended laugh, but every banker in the room knew how true it was.

"I've done business with Delbert for more than thirty years," White said. "I've learned that when he makes up his mind to take on a project, he won't take no for an answer. He has total confidence in his ability.

"When Delbert first told me about the North Overton development project, I told him he was crazy. I advised him that he shouldn't risk the ranch on this project, but told him if he decided to do it, I'd help him."

White believes that when Delbert has a vision for a project, he will get it done.

"Delbert's vision, his willingness to tackle the big projects, and his relationships with financial people around the country is what separates him from other developers," White said.

"And what most people don't know is how big a part Carolyn has been in the company's success. She's a class act."

CHAPTER 6

RECLAIMING A NEIGHBORHOOD, 1999-2003

The "war zones" a the North Overton demolition area was described.

When Delbert McDougal decided to redevelop the North Overton area, he had three broad goals:
- Reclaim the neighborhood from deterioration
- Compliment the growth of Texas Tech University
- Contribute to the revitalization of Downtown Lubbock

Beginning in January 1999, McDougal began acquiring empty lots and properties in North Overton. He also put many option contracts on properties, and was often able to do so with a $100 fee.

"Early on, the project seemed monumental," Delbert said. "We began with the people who owned the most property."

"By approaching the large apartment owners, we were able to acquire about 40 percent of the property in the first 90 days. Most sellers were elated to sell to us. They feared they would never be able to sell their properties.

"We thought about trying to buy all this surreptitiously, but I decided not to take that approach, with the exception of a few major properties on the west side for which we had acquired options."

Now, it was time to put together financing.

Delbert initiated discussions with several local banks, and with Fannie Mae, the publicly traded entity that provides mortgages for low- to middle-income families.

Three local banks agreed to an initial $8-million loan to get the project kicked off. They were American State Bank, Plains Capital Bank, and City Bank. The quoted rate for this money was prime plus 1, approximately 7 percent.

"As I moved forward," Delbert said, "I talked to Fannie Mae, and also planned to put together an investment group.

"I expected to bring in a major brokerage house from New York or Florida. I knew I would have to pay them a fairly high interest rate, but they would not be partners in the deal. I wanted to avoid taking on partners if at all possible."

Financing the project in this way allowed Delbert to take the project on in small bites. Under this scenario, he planned to work out agreements with people in concept, then stage the closings over time until he had it all purchased.

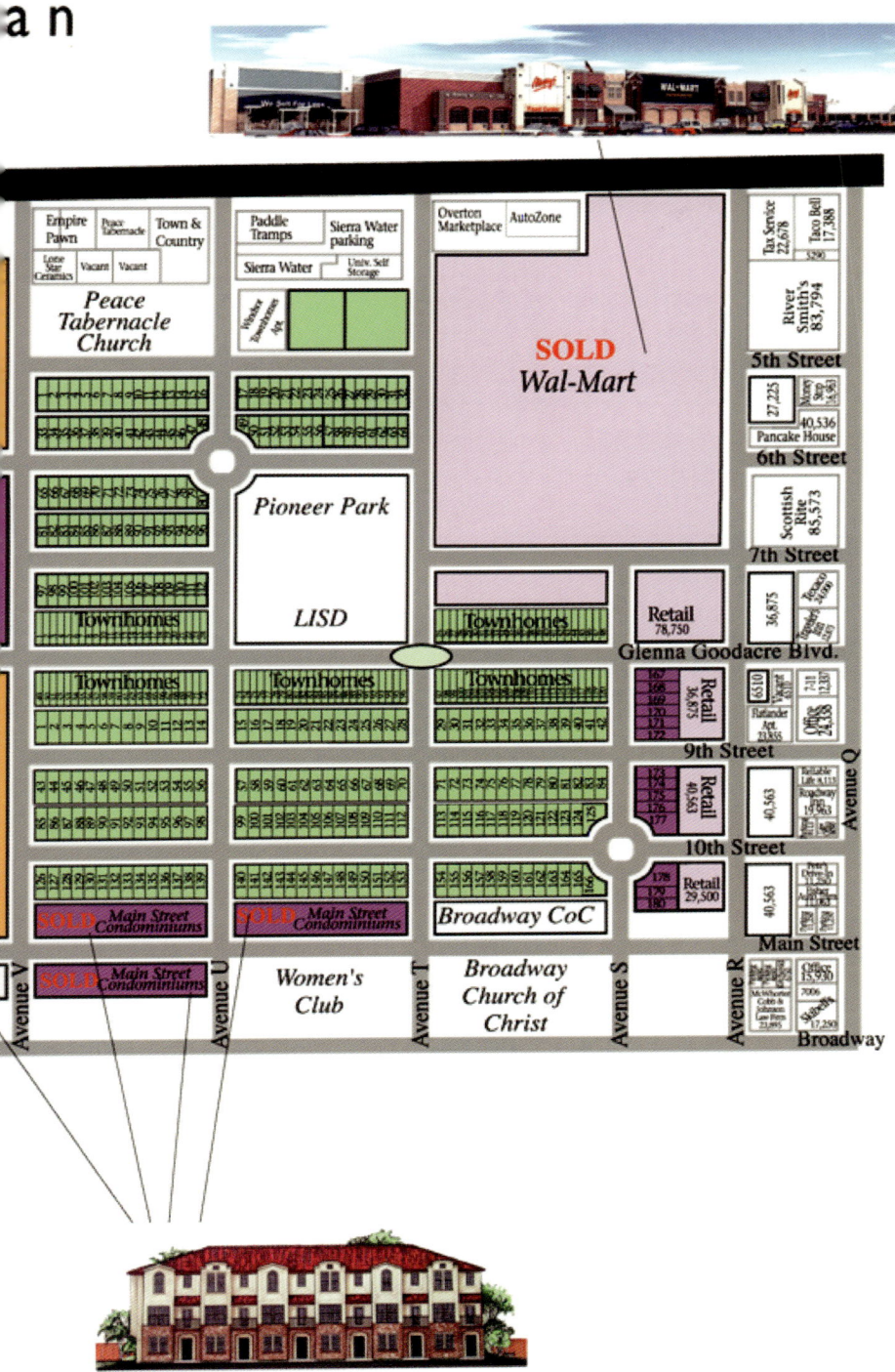

McDougal's Master plan for Overton Park, in it's "near-final" form.

But McDougal learned that sellers were interested in moving more quickly.

"I had to increase my financing and acquire large tracts of land," Delbert said. "Buyers needed to be certain about the whole project, not just the land they wanted to build on. They needed to see that the decayed properties adjacent to them were also gone. "

McDougal's conversations with Fannie Mae focused on a $12.5-million loan. But he also knew that Fannie Mae's participation would bring a lot of red tape, and came with many regulations regarding the people who bought homes in the project.

"It only took a couple of meetings to realize that we weren't going to be able to do business together. Had we been able to work a deal, it looked as though we could've borrowed the money at prime plus a half-percent.

"The Fannie Mae folks also brought up the idea of joining us as a partner, but I was not interested in that."

"I also got the sense that the folks at Fannie Mae didn't believe I could accomplish my plan in Overton," Delbert said.

More North Overton housing.

RESIDENT'S CONCERNS

For the residents of North Overton, news of McDougal's plans to acquire and level their homes left many of them worried.

In spite of public assurances from McDougal and City of Lubbock officials that homeowners would not be forced out of their homes, rumors to the contrary flew around the neighborhood.

Residents in apartment buildings felt especially vulnerable, and rightly so. As McDougal closed the deals, apartment owners notified residents when they'd have to move.

To help ease their fears, McDougal assigned a team of staffers to work with displaced residents to help them find new housing.

At the same time, several groups of concerned citizens began to organize and meet. Doris Fletcher, president of the North Overton Neighborhood Association, asked Delbert if he would meet with the residents to answer their questions.

He readily agreed.

AN ANGRY MEETING

On August 10, 1999, less than a month after the announcement, the McDougal family attended a North Overton resident's meeting at Ramirez Elementary school, located in the heart of the neighborhood.

Carolyn remembers the scene vividly.

"When we arrived," she said, "there were people walking from every direction to the school. I made the comment that they must be having a PTA meeting.

"But I soon learned they were all coming to this meeting. The room was packed. The Neighborhood Association had put fliers on every door."

"We counted nearly two hundred people at the meeting. I sat next to my son Mike as Doris introduced Delbert.

"After Delbert made some opening comments about his plan, a lady stood up to speak. She went on an emotional and angry tirade against the project, and shook her fist at Delbert.

"I began to get nervous and looked around a couple of times and saw many angry faces. Mike suggested that I stop turning around. I kicked myself for not thinking of arranging to have a security officer in attendance."

After listening to the first speaker, Doris Fletcher took the floor.

She addressed the crowd, asking them to keep themselves under control. She reminded them that she invited Delbert to the meeting, and they owed him the courtesy of being civil.

The meeting continued. There was much anger in the room, but the remaining speakers were less hostile. Delbert listened to the concerns and answered them.

He explained to homeowners he would be offering to buy their properties. If they didn't want to sell, they didn't have to.

He cautioned them that there would be much construction and inconvenience for the next five to seven years, but he would do everything possible to lessen the impact on the residents.

For those who chose to stay, when the project was finished, their property was going to be worth more, and their neighborhood would be safer.

In closing, McDougal urged residents to listen to his offers to buy their property, visit with his staff on relocation possibilities, and weigh their options before assuming worst-case scenarios.

Several McDougal employees had come to the meeting, and they all joined Delbert and Carolyn as they walked a block from the meeting to their car.

"I was still quite fearful," Carolyn said.

"When we got in the car and drove away, I asked Delbert again why we were putting up with this aggravation at this point in our lives. We didn't need it."

But Carolyn knew that once Delbert starts something, he sees it through. He wasn't going to back off the project.

GOOD NEWS, GOOD NEWS

Before the project was a year old, Delbert was getting more good news than he had hoped for. Potential sellers were beating a path to his door, eager to get rid of their properties.

He had a very good problem. Things were going better than planned. But he'd need a lot more money right away.

As he had done so often during a project he had to adjust his plan. He believed he would need to expand his $12-million loan up to $30 million.

"My original plan," Delbert said, "was that as we acquired property, we could go back to the banks for more money where they'd have a lien on properties that I acquired.

One of the first properties McDougal bought was from the father of country music singer-songwriter Mac Davis. He owned fifteen rent houses close to University Avenue. Next, he closed on University Arms Apartments, and with that he had enough property to start developing his first full block of commercially zoned property.

After the announcement, things moved quickly. He bought 48 houses from one individual. There were only 2 or 3 single-home owners in the western part of the neighborhood.

The McDougals did continue to hear skepticism and concerns from the community. Part of it was lingering distrust from the resident's meeting, and some of it was being fueled by others interested in acquiring some of the property in North Overton, in hopes they could in turn resell it to McDougal for a tidy profit.

"We tried to keep everyone informed," Delbert said. "But we couldn't stay ahead of all the rumors for the longest time."

Delbert finally told all his staff not to worry about what was heard on the street or said in the media.

"Our goal was to offer property owners a fair deal for their property" Delbert said.

"Then, we worked to help those who sold their property to us find suitable housing in other neighborhoods."

McDougal staffers understood the implications of the area they were working in.

"North Overton was a very dangerous place during this time," said McDougal's investment analyst Jerry Roberson.

"On more than one occasion, I was threatened when I was in the area," Jerry said. "Utility companies often requested police protection when working in the area.

"People who just saw the area from one of the bordering streets didn't always comprehend how bad the situation had gotten in there."

The ability to return the North Overton neighborhood to a safe and quality living environment was at the core of McDougal's interest in taking on the project.

This was where he began his housing business. This was the center of the downtown, university, and medical communities. This project had to be done.

One of a number of North Overton houses moved to another location.

THE BANKING COALITION CHANGES

When lining up financing, McDougal first approached American State Bank, because they were located just a few blocks from North Overton. He believed they had the most to gain by its redevelopment.

He also brought in two other banks that he'd had relationships with, Plains Capital Bank and City Bank. Between the three banks, Delbert secured an initial loan of $8 million, which he expected to carry him through the first year of the project, while he began negotiations with a number of potential equity partners on various pieces of property.

"The $8-million loan was the largest we'd ever taken on," Mike McDougal said. We referred to it as "The Big Loan" around the office.

During this period of frenetic acquisitions, the value of having an in house realtor was never more readily apparent.

"We'd send a realtor out to work a block of property," Delbert said. Normally that involved ten to twelve houses. We guessed it would take six months to get all those purchased, but they were coming back in six weeks with all the contracts signed."

This completely changed McDougal's financial needs. As the project picked up steam Delbert needed to have a larger line of financing. He met with all three banks to discuss the changing nature of the project.

McDougal laid out the good news about their ability to purchase more of the property, and let them know he would need more money.

He projected additional cash needs of $13 million, increasing the total loan from $8 to $21 million.

"During the course of the renegotiation it became evident that it would be difficult to finalize a new loan agreement without putting up additional collateral," Delbert said. "I was not willing to do that.

"I felt the banks should let this property stand on its own without having to commit my other properties for security. They also wanted to increase the interest rate by a point.

"I was disappointed in the banks' response, because we all knew going into the deal that a project of this magnitude would take many twists and turns. I needed financial partners who were going to be with me through the entire project.

Shortly after McDougal returned to his office, Mike Liner, the president of City Bank called. His bank was one of the three that had made the initial $8 million loan.

He wanted to reiterate that City Bank believed in the project, and offered to handle all Delbert's future financing needs in North Overton.

City Bank is a relatively young bank. Started in 1993, it had grown quickly in Lubbock and West Texas, amassing nearly $80 million in capital.

"I thought that Delbert had a great idea regarding this important neighborhood," City Bank President Mike Liner said. "I've been to most large college campuses across the country, and I've never seen the opportunity to create that much prime vacant land across the street from a major university.

"When Delbert showed me his Overton plans, I was very excited. I told him I wanted the opportunity to buy the first piece of property in the project to put a bank down there.

"Because of the recent growth of students at Texas Tech, and my confidence in Delbert as a skilled developer, I had no question that this project was going to be a huge success.

"The only question was Delbert's having adequate financing to be able to pay for it all."

Mike Liner, president and CEO of City Bank in Lubbock.

When the project accelerated, some saw it as a cause for concern. Liner saw it as an opportunity, and told Delbert if he'd let their bank handle all the project's future needs, he would get whatever funding was needed."

This was music to Delbert's ears. But he knew that City Bank didn't have a large enough portfolio to allow them to make this large a loan to one project. How would they handle it?

Few financial institutions can set aside $30 million to handle a project of this size. City Bank had developed relationships with more than thirty small correspondent banks in the region that were looking for good loans. Most of these banks are located in small and medium sized agricultural communities within a few hours' drive to Lubbock. More importantly, they were in the market for investment opportunities outside agriculture.

Mike Liner knew that the officers of these banks were familiar enough with Lubbock, and would understand the importance of this project.

Mike told Delbert he wanted the opportunity to bring these bankers to Lubbock to see the vision and the property. Delbert was intrigued.

"It took a leap of faith on Delbert's part," Mike Liner said. "I didn't have $30 million lined up at that time."

"I still had it in the back of my mind that I would have to go to major financers at some point," Delbert said.

"But City Bank was very aggressive, wanting to finance the whole project. They were completely sold on the project, both as an investment for their stockholders, and the benefits to the community."

After a number of meetings over the next several weeks, McDougal and Liner had an agreement.

The original $8 million loan with the three banks stayed in place. City Bank took over exclusive financing for the remainder of the project, up to $50 million.

McDougal signed personal guarantees for the initial loan, and used acquired property as collateral as the loan increased.

"As we moved forward, I even met with bank examiners at their request," Delbert said.

"I've never heard of bank examiners meeting with a developer. Since that one meeting, we've not had any further questions asked about our progress."

"In addition to the coalition of smaller banks, City Bank also has relationships with a number of large banks that we wanted to approach for participation," Mike Liner said.

"As the project moved forward, I brought in about forty banks to take some investment participation in the North Overton project.

"We are very proud to have been a part of this incredible project."

McDougal and Liner met weekly to get updates on the progress on offers, contracts, demolition, and cash flow needs.

Delbert's real estate agents would offer contracts with ninety day closings. But often, the seller wanted to close immediately. That forced Delbert to act quickly.

The cash flow schedules changed almost daily during the first two years. But those changes were being driven by good opportunities, not problems.

"For example," Mike Liner said, "one day Delbert called to tell me that instead of needing $5 million in the upcoming month, he was going to need $10 million. And by the way, he would also need $3 million tomorrow.

"At City Bank, we have about $80 million in capital, and we're allowed to loan up to 25 percent of our certified surplus, or about $20 million. Of course, we don't want to loan any one entity too large a portion of our portfolio. That's too much exposure for the bank.

"On several occasions when there would be a cash crunch with the project, I've gone to my board to ask to be allowed to exceed our self-imposed lending limit for a short period of time.

"I had to jump through some hoops, but we were able to meet our obligations to Delbert. He gave us a great opportunity, so getting enough financing was now my problem, not his."

McDougal initially thought he could buy land in North Overton for an average of $4 per square foot, and thought it would take something around $17 million to acquire enough of the property to put together the commercial side of the project.

"This scope of commercial opportunity next to Texas Tech hadn't occurred in Lubbock for a long time," said Jerry Roberson.

"We underestimated its value quite a bit. We were told by others that this was the largest

More North Overton housing.

privately-funded urban renewal project in the country."

At the time the project was announced, Delbert believed the most expensive land that had ever been purchased in Lubbock was at Nineteenth Street and University Avenue, about a half-mile away. A hotel-suites property was built there in 1999 and the land sold for $7.90 per square foot.

By 2005, McDougal was selling land less than a mile away for commercial use at $25 per square foot.

The price for apartment development in North Overton saw a similar jump in value. Land for apartments reached more than $12.50 per foot in 2005, which was nearly ten times more than the usual range of $0.75 to $1.50 per foot paid in Lubbock before the project started.

There was another major initiative during this period. Delbert was negotiating with Texas Tech University and a state agency to partner on a luxury hotel and teaching facility.

Texas Tech has a well known Restaurant and Hotel Institutional Management (RHIM) program, and they were interested in the new hotel close to the campus that could serve as a teaching facility.

Lubbock leaders had long yearned for a four-star hotel, and McDougal considered it one of his most important objectives for the redevelopment.

In spite of years of work, the deal never matured.

HELPING WITH RELOCATION

McDougal's goal in purchasing homes was to reach a fair deal for both parties, and that sellers were helped to secure adequate housing somewhere else.

In the case of displaced apartment dwellers, his company created an apartment referral service to help with relocation. In some cases, renters were offered higher-priced apartments that McDougal owned, at the same monthly rent as they were paying in North Overton.

"In the case of one disabled lady," said Jerry Roberson, "we built her a wheelchair ramp where she relocated.

In another case, the company helped relocate a woman to New York, where her mother lived.

Doris Fletcher, the president of the North Overton Neighborhood Association finally decided to accept McDougal's offer on her house.

"Once people saw what they could afford in a new neighborhood, they began to sell their homes to us," Delbert said.

"We handled everything. All they had to tell us was where they wanted us to put the furniture in their new home."

DEMOLITION & ABATEMENT

As McDougal began buying properties in North Overton by the dozens, those who elected to continue living there began to realize the impact the project would have on them.

Vacant houses and apartments were boarded up awaiting demolition, which took some time to accomplish.

Several fires were set in vacant homes, and the pressure on McDougal to step up the demolition increased.

"Our initial thought was not to tear anything down for a couple of years," Delbert said.

"We wanted to get it all bought first. That changed, because the people who were purchasing tracts wanted the structures around their new development removed before they closed their deals.

"They wanted to know that we were not going to uncover environmental issues or ground contamination issues in our demolition that could impact their property."

Rumors began to surface that McDougal wasn't concerned about the arsonist, because it would save money on demolition.

In fact, just the opposite was true. A burned house costs more to demolish and remove because asbestos still has to be abated, and the cost of sifting through burned rubble is higher.

But McDougal knew he had to ramp up the demolition and clearing operation.

"Once we boarded a house up," Delbert said, "we had to have it removed in a certain timeframe.

"Interestingly, the police like for empty houses to be boarded, because it makes it harder for criminals to get in them and offer them a place to hide. The fire department, however, doesn't like boarded houses, because it makes it difficult for them to see in and assess the fire, and if there are people inside."

Because North Overton quickly had such a huge number of vacant houses, Delbert worked out a compromise with city and state officials to knock the houses down, and then systematically remove the rubble in an environmentally friendly way.

By knocking down large numbers of houses, he was able to speed up the recycling process by doing the sorting and collecting on site, then moving the various recyclable products to their final destination.

"It took our demolition crews about a year to get all the rubble sorted and cleared out," Delbert said. "Almost every house out there had some type of asbestos in it."

"As we moved along, it became apparent we couldn't wait for the demolition to be handled on site. We insisted that the company start recycling the materials during the demolition process, then move the partially-separated materials off-site to complete the process."

This helped speed up the demolition and recycling process, which was necessary to match the growing demand for lots to be cleared so new construction could begin.

McDougal also found it was easier and more cost effective to permit and abate asbestos a block at a time, rather than a house at a time. So he began planning demolition in blocks, whenever possible.

"This part of the project held the most surprises for us," Delbert said.

"We thought we'd just work in one area at a time. But we basically had to buy, demo, clear, and build simultaneously throughout the 325 acres.

McDougal worked with R. E. "Corky" Matthews, a local demolition contractor and recycler, to do everything possible to be environmentally friendly.

"I was very proud of our recycling operation," Delbert said. "We were able to reuse about 95 percent of the more than 900 structures that were torn down.

While the recycling slowed the process down, it also meant that only five percent of all the demolition debris was transported to the City landfill.

Once McDougal got through the year-long demo phase to catch up with what he'd torn down, approximately sixty percent of the commercial lots had been cleared and readied for sale.

Outside developers were knocking at his door to buy property at this point.

THE DAY THE COUNTRY STOOD STILL

In September 1997, Lubbock's Reese Air Force Base was closed, along with a number of others in a Pentagon cost-cutting effort.

On Tuesday morning, September 11, 2001, Delbert McDougal was scheduled for a meeting in Washington D.C. at the Pentagon.

Delbert was serving as chair of the Reese Technology Center, which had become one of the few success stories of military base reuse. Delbert and Eric Williams, CEO of the RTC were to have met with Air Force brass in D.C. on 9/11 to discuss some issues relating to reuse of the closed air base. The meeting had been cancelled just two days prior to the attack on the Pentagon.

"It was an odd feeling to watch the news that day and know that at the time of this terrible tragedy in American History, I had appointments in the Pentagon that day," Delbert said.

But McDougal never felt the fallout from the terrorist attack would have a significant impact on the Overton project.

"Like everyone else in the country, we were stunned by what happened," Delbert said.

"A friend asked me how this disaster was going to affect our project. I told him the fact is that Lubbock and Texas Tech were going to continue to grow on a long term basis. And this was a long term project.

"Wars can impact the cost of money, or the cost of materials, but you can't do a project of this nature worried about world events.

"You make decisions each day based on what you have in front of you, and move forward."

McDougal's intuition again proved correct. From 2001 to 2004, total enrollment at Texas Tech increased more than 10 percent, from 25,573 to 28,325.

THE TAX INCREMENT FINANCE DISTRICT

In late 2001, Rob Allison, who headed the City's Development Division began discussing a growing mechanism to self-fund development projects like the one in North Overton. In response, the Lubbock City Council approved a Tax Increment Finance district (TIF) for the development.

In a TIF, the current property taxes collected from a given area are set as a base line. The property value in Overton at that time was $28 million. Taxes from that base amount continue to flow to the local taxing entities, so there is no loss in revenue to the governmental service providers.

As new properties were built in the district, the tax base increases, and additional money is generated. Those revenues above the base line amount are held in a fund for public improvements within the designated TIF.

These funds would allow the City to fund needed infrastructure improvements in the area. With newly paved streets and utilities, developers and builders will have more incentive to upgrade and build, which will help raise property values.

By agreeing to give up increased revenues from property value growth in the area for a set number of years, taxing entities are betting that they'll realize tax revenue increases down the road.

The TIF was approved by the City and County, and a nine-member board was named to oversee spending of TIF funding.

The North Overton TIF was set up for a maximum thirty year time frame. But if all the public infrastructure is paid off prior to that time, the TIF dissolves, and all tax revenues flow to the local taxing authorities.

As new buildings and commerce began moving into North Overton, utility companies took the opportunity to upgrade old infrastructure that was in constant need of repair.

DESIGN STANDARDS

McDougal wanted the new homes in North Overton to have the look of the early 1900s urban living style that characterized the neighborhood when it was built.

"Houses will be closer to the street, unlike typical homes built today," Delbert said. "We moved the driveways and garages to the back of the lots, with entries from the alley.

"We wanted most of the houses to have front porches and higher pitched roofs, which were reflective of the style when the neighborhood was first built.

New homes in old styles, under construction in 2007

New homes under construction in Overton Park, 2007.

McDougal selected two architectural firms to participate in the design of the project. Humphrey & Partners Architects from Dallas, Texas and Parkhill, Smith & Cooper from Lubbock. They created a mix of building styles that were reflective of the era, from which builders can select.

As the project gained steam, people started thinking creatively about what they could do in the area. A good example was seen with the Lubbock Independent School District and the staff at an elementary school located in the heart of North Overton.

A SCHOOL IS REBORN

The neighborhood decay had also redefined Ramirez Elementary School, a public magnet school located near the center of the neighborhood.

Created in the 1980s, the Lubbock Independent School District elementary had eight hundred students at its peak. But enrollment had dwindled down to fewer than two hundred students.

As the revitalization project began to tear down and remove most of the homes in the neighborhood, the school saw the challenges ahead.

"We were excited about the changes proposed for North Overton," said Joann Newman, Multicultural Events and University Coordinator with Ramirez Elementary.

"But knew we had to begin looking at what we could do to best position Ramirez Elementary for the changes that were literally taking place all around us.

"Because of our proximity to Texas Tech, we partnered with the College of Education during the initial planning stages. It was during these discussions with the university and Lubbock Independent School District that the possibility of creating a campus charter school came into focus.

The campus charter school concept allowed Ramirez faculty to have some creative flexibility while meeting the needs of the changing neighborhood. Campus charters remain under the direction of the Board Trustees and adhere to state and federal accountability measures.

This involved both Texas Tech education students, along with local businesses partnering with the school to teach business concepts as well as citizenship and leadership. Parental Involvement is also a key to campus charter schools.

A new mission statement for the school was created.

The Mission of Ramirez Charter School is to launch successful life long learners within a supportive educational environment that promotes leadership, excellence, creativity, problem solving, collaboration, and community.

"Parents, teachers, and staff began marketing

❖

Ground breaking for The Centre in 2004.

the new campus charter school through the media, by one-on-one visits in homes, renting booths at the local flea markets on weekends, and manning tables at shopping malls," Newman said.

"We participated in parades, fiestas, and attended meetings all over town. Our staff would speak anywhere we could find a group willing to listen. This personal, face-to-face marketing was the key to getting the word out about what we were creating at Ramirez.

"Our students' parents were key to this effort."

When Ramirez Charter School opened its doors at the beginning of August 2004, the children began flooding in. Ramirez jumped from fewer than 200 students to 411 within the first weeks of operation during the fall of 2004. Fall 2005 enrollment was 442.

The student body now comes from all parts of town and other neighboring school districts.

Ramirez also began offering after-school enrichment opportunities for students, with more than twenty programs. Children participate in a variety of challenging arts, exercise, and mind-enriching programs once school is officially over.

These popular programs keep children engaged in positive learning and social activities, while their parents are working and not at home.

Excitement in the rebirth of Ramirez Charter Elementary is shared by the faculty and staff.

"I have taught in the public schools for 18 years, and I have never been around a group of teachers so involved with their students and each other," Newman said.

"Ramirez Charter School and North Overton have changed so much. Once again, they're alive!"

Lubbock ISD school superintendent Wayne Havens echoes the feelings from Ramirez.

"I think one of the most exciting parts of the Overton redevelopment effort is the fact that we have Ramirez Charter School in that area. Our partnership with Texas Tech University has really created a campus environment that is very challenging for the students presently enrolled and will certainly meet the needs of future students who will choose to move into homes in North Overton."

THE FIRST DEVELOPMENT

As properties were bought and cleared, McDougal made his first development deal in North Overton. Ironically, it was for apartments to be built and owned by The Dinerstein

Company, a Houston apartment developer that builds throughout the country.

"Our plan going in was to keep about thirty percent of the properties in Overton to develop ourselves," Delbert said.

"We would offer the rest of the property to other developers and builders. We used the profits from the property we sold to pay interest and work our loans down."

The Dinerstein Group, a fifty-year-old apartment developer that specializes in building next to college campuses built the first new construction in North Overton.

Until November 2004, Dinerstein was the largest off-campus student housing company in the country, when they sold the majority of their assets.

They have built more than 40,000 apartments around the country, in addition to 22,000 student housing beds.

Like McDougal Properties, The Dinerstein Company is a family business. President Jack Dinerstein worked in the company for thirty-three years and took over the business from his father, Bill.

"Since the beginning of my involvement in the apartment industry, I've been aware of Delbert McDougal and his Lubbock companies," Jack Dinerstein said.

"Delbert is known throughout the country as a leader in the industry.

"Our company looked at Texas Tech as a potential for additional student housing, during the university's growth spurt in the late 1990s.

"We were excited about the prospects of Tech's growth, but at the time, North Overton was a no-man's land. The area was run down and too dangerous for students, in our estimation.

"When Delbert contacted us a few years later to say he was going to redevelop the entire area, I was skeptical. To be more candid, I did not think it could be done. I've seen many developers across the country attempt to change the makeup of an entire submarket and fail.

"A perfect example is in Houston, where our company is located. A company redeveloped more than five thousand rundown apartments around the Houston Intercontinental Airport about 8 to 10 years ago. The end result was that the area is still plagued with declining properties and high crime. In essence, many of the same problems returned, and the area is rapidly declining. It was a colossal failure.

"Redevelopment is not easy to do. Lots of very good developers have lost money trying.

"Delbert did it the right way. He's very organized and methodical. He is a very bright and determined man.

"I'm not sure there was anybody in the country that could do what Delbert did in Lubbock."

The Dinerstein Company brought the first new construction to North Overton in July

An aerial view of new student housing in the revitalized area.

2002, when they began work on a 240-unit, three-story apartment community. At that time, there were still many empty lots and dilapidated houses sitting around the neighborhood. But students responded very well to the project and it quickly filled up.

A year later, Dinerstein built another similar sized property and began construction on a third student housing project. When finished in 2005, Dinerstein built housing for nearly 3,000 students in North Overton.

"None of this would've been possible without Delbert's vision, and his ability to pull it off," Jack Dinerstein said. "I've not seen this magnitude of development done anywhere, and we're active in twenty-six states.

"Needless to say, I'm a huge fan of Delbert McDougal."

In 2004, City Bank followed up their desire to have the first commercial development in North Overton by starting construction on a two story bank at the corner of University Avenue and Glenna Goodacre Boulevard. The Spanish renaissance design is punctuated with a fifty-one-foot clock tower with chimes.

"We're very pleased to have a prime location in the North Overton Project," said City Bank's Mike Liner.

"Our building reflects the architecture of both the campus and the historic nature of Overton. Our clock tower chimes are heard on campus as well as in the neighborhood, signaling our pride to have played a part in this historic redevelopment."

INFRASTRUCTURE ISSUES

The utility replacement phase was also a challenging management issue for McDougal, and required constant attention.

The North Overton master plan called for placing all utilities underground, but during the replacement process, electric and telephone service had to be maintained by moving and patching existing above ground wire.

"We had to coordinate with two electric utility companies, two phone companies, one gas company, and one cable company," Delbert said.

"All this was going on in the midst of existing neighborhoods, large areas of demolition, and simultaneous construction."

Because McDougal was moving so fast with demolition, utilities had to start "bridging" their service. That would allow them to keep power to existing customers while they laid in new underground wires for the whole area.

"At one point," Delbert noted, "we couldn't get one of the companies to take their old poles away.

"The wires were already off, but the fact the poles were still on the property held up a survey for three weeks.

"The purchaser wanted to show an unobstructed topography in the survey. Even though the poles were going down, the fact they were still there held up our ability to close on a piece of property by several weeks.

"This was an especially challenging piece of the redevelopment puzzle. It was much more difficult that I expected."

There are always unknowns in a project of this magnitude. The next surprise came when McDougal started replacing water and sewer lines.

Delbert got a call one day telling him that they'd just found out that most of the water lines in North Overton were coated with asbestos. This necessitated a more costly abatement problem than expected.

The solution was to cut the old pipe into twenty foot sections, wrap them to keep the asbestos from flying off in chunks, and truck the pipe sections off to a different location, where they were properly disposed.

"We had to do all this because we were buying alleys, and thus, whatever was underneath them," Delbert said.

"If we hadn't been buying the alleys, it would've been the City's problem. In every alley, we had to deal with underground telephone, gas, cable, and overhead electric lines.

"This was by far the most difficult part of the process. We were moving so fast, it was overwhelming to the utility companies, as well as our contractors."

Lubbock has two electric utilities, competing door to door for customers in almost every block of the city.

McDougal had planned on using just one electric underground cable and let the two electric utilities work out a sharing arrangement for their customers.

But the electric utilities were unable to reach

agreement on a sharing plan, and dual sets of electric wires had to be relocated.

"Coordinating the new utility infrastructure was much harder than all of the prior pieces of the project," Delbert said.

"We planned to do the project in phases, which would've been easier. But we couldn't pass up the opportunity to purchase properties when they were available.

"And after we owned vacant properties, the community concerns regarding crime and safety made it impossible not to proceed through the whole area.

"It was a good problem to have, but it proved to be a challenge."

McDougal was contacted by other cities and developers weekly, to get his advice on their projects. He occasionally traveled to other cities to take a look and help them assess their needs.

"Cities are surprised when I tell them coordinating the utilities is the most difficult part," Delbert said.

Zoning is often a sticky issue in redevelopments. Property owners within three hundred feet of all zone change requests are offered the opportunity to support or oppose all zone changes when they are considered by the City Council.

In North Overton's case, zoning was less of an issue. By the time McDougal began the zoning changes, he owned almost all the properties around the proposed zone change. As properties began to sell and go through a rezoning process, there were very few protests.

McDougal believed that when looking at the project before the redevelopment began, people couldn't see the forest for the trees. They approached North Overton as it looked, and how difficult it would be to repair, remodel, and restore.

Delbert's approach was to visualize the area as a clean tract.

"The end result is that an area that had large pockets of blight and crime is now one of the most valuable pieces of real estate in Lubbock.

"Once I had my plan in mind, and put it on a piece of paper, I knew it was going to happen. Failure was not an option."

After the project was well underway, McDougal ran across his copy of the 1986 Overton Revitalization Plan, put together by Texas Tech's Dr. Peng with the assistance of a number of community leaders. He hadn't seen it in nearly fifteen years.

He was interested to see how his plan compared with the proposal laid out conceptually years ago. It was remarkably close.

THE CENTRE-PIECE

In 2001, two years after McDougal made his announcement to begin the North Overton

The Centre under construction in 2004.

PHOTO COURTESY OF CHILDRESS PHOTOGRAPHY.

project, he and his family went to an apartment association convention in Houston, Texas.

They had to opportunity to see a newly built upscale apartment complex that highly successful developers Jim Hepfner and Tom Day recently completed.

The McDougals were immediately impressed, and knew this type of property would work in Lubbock.

"We took the basic concept of this Houston property," Mike McDougal said, expanded it and added retail to the first floor."

Mike McDougal called their architect and asked him to look at the property. The architect took the basic concept and added ideas from other innovative multi-use projects, and produced the design for what would become a centerpiece multifamily project of the development.

At the news conference introducing plans for The Centre in September 2002, Delbert McDougal officially renamed the neighborhood. Honoring the memory of its pioneer physician-founder, Dr. M. C. Overton, he christened the new neighborhood Overton Park.

Nan Overton West, one of Dr. Overton's daughters attended the event and praised McDougal for his vision in returning the beauty and vitality to the neighborhood.

A year later, McDougal broke ground on The Centre at Overton Park. The facility is a two-block, $30 million mixed-use property that features 277 upscale apartment homes with street level retail space. Residents have inside parking on the same floor where they live, while retail customers enjoy covered parking on the ground floor.

GROWING IN ALL DIRECTIONS

While the Overton Park project was dominating McDougal's attention during the 1990s, a number of his other housing development projects were taking off in north and west Lubbock.

McDougal's property portfolio doubled in size between 1992 and 2001, reaching a total of more than five thousand apartments in five west Texas cities.

GOING FISHING

Not long after Delbert announced his Overton project, he joined Mike Liner, president of City Bank, and another local business man on a deep sea fishing trip off the coast of Mexico.

"The boat can get pretty rocky in the ocean," Mike Liner said. "I always take medicine to keep from getting seasick and ruining a great day of fishing.

"The three of us boarded a boat that left San Diego one evening to get us to the fishing area over night.

"After bouncing around all night, we got up early to start fishing our way back to the coast. The seas were still rough that morning.

"I was feeling a little sick, and declined breakfast, but not Delbert. He ate a huge breakfast.

"I took some more Dramamine, and got my gear together. By the time I got up to the deck, Delbert was already in the front of the boat, sitting in his seat with his feet up on the railing. He was smoking a cigar, and had his line in the water, happy as a clam.

"It occurred to me then that Delbert has a special quality to handle pressure. Here's a man who just took on $12 million in debt with a lot more on the way, and could leave it all behind for a few days to go fishing.

"He was able to put aside the financial pressures that would've made most men throw up on solid ground, much less on choppy seas.

"Delbert is the most optimistic person I know. He never thinks negatively, or calls me with problems he doesn't know how to handle."

Cool as a cucumber: Delbert on his fishing trip with City Bank.

The new Wal-Mart Supercenter with The Centre and Jones/AT&T Stadium in the background. The store opened in the summer of 2006.

CHAPTER 7

REDEVELOPMENT LESSONS, 2003-2006

Broken down to its most basic parts, neighborhood redevelopment projects consist of planning, acquisition, demolition/rehabilitation, infrastructure replacement, sales, zoning, and construction.

In a normal multi-use development project, the first phase is single family homes. Retail and commercial will follow the entrance of residents. The last phase of a traditional project would be multi-family housing.

In the Overton Park redevelopment, the order of construction was flipped. Multi-family housing led, commercial followed, and single family housing was the last developed.

The first properties developed were apartments, because of the great need for them in proximity to the Tech campus.

"In the master plan, we knew we'd start the development on University Avenue," Delbert said. "We then began to move eastward toward downtown."

Plans for commercial development included retail shops along University Avenue and eventually, along Avenue Q. The first to be marketed were along University, and in the first floor of McDougal's multi-use complex, known as The Centre at Overton Park.

Discussions also began about a four-star hotel and a number of restaurants, all to be located across from Texas Tech and next to the Centre.

What was not in the plans was a "big box" retailer, like Wal-Mart.

WAL-MART CALLS

All eyes in Lubbock were on McDougal during the early stages of the Overton Park project. There was still a fair amount of skepticism about his ability to pull it off.

But the Overton Park project was also garnering attention outside Lubbock. The country's major chain operations keep a close eye on local development trends. Without fanfare, they visit growing communities to look for opportunities.

On several occasions, Wal-Mart's real estate executives quietly came to Lubbock to look at Overton Park and other properties. With two stores already thriving in the community, they were looking to add two more.

They didn't contact McDougal until they had scouted out possible locations, and completed their market research and engineering plans.

"Tom Hudson, Wal-Mart's Fort Worth real estate representative called me to discuss buying a piece of property on the northeast corner of the project," Delbert said, "I told them I doubted a Wal-Mart would work at Overton Park.

"It had nothing to do with any concerns about the retail operation. This part of town needed more retail outlets, and that need would grow as we began bringing people back into the downtown area.

"My concern was architectural. Based on all the Wal-Mart stores I'd seen, I didn't see them as an appropriate fit for the style of redevelopment we wanted to build."

But Hudson assured McDougal they had new store designs that could fit his architectural guidelines in Overton Park.

Their engineers had already picked a specific site on the north east corner of the project, and they wanted to meet to show him their plans.

When the Wal-Mart team sat down with McDougal, their first question was to ask him who was handling the financing for the Overton Park project.

"I told them a coalition of local banks," Delbert said.

"They thought I was joking. They couldn't believe that there was enough money in West Texas to take on a project of this size.

"I assured them it was no joke. It was a question I answered frequently when discussing purchases in the project. Every one of the out-of-down developers I worked with found it hard to believe."

With Wal-Mart's willingness to build in the historic style of the neighborhood, McDougal looked at their plan, and began to calculate what changes in the project's master plan would be needed to accommodate the store's operation.

"Our first issue was to find a way to fence off the back side of the store so that housing next to the store would have visual and noise protection," Delbert said.

"We also had to design the delivery truck route to keep the commercial vehicles away from the nearby housing and elementary school.

"I began to see that this deal could work within the overall concept of what I was trying to build."

Wal-Mart was sold on what was happening in Overton Park, and they believed the people in north and east Lubbock were underserved with retail opportunities.

McDougal agreed. He contacted City planners to get their view of the Wal-Mart project of this nature in Overton Park. They were delighted the nation's largest retailer was interested in having a huge presence in downtown Lubbock. They encouraged Delbert to continue the conversations as long as Wal-Mart would agree to the architectural plans for the area.

"Not long after I began discussing a sale with Wal-Mart," Delbert said, "I got a call from a legal firm in another city. The lawyer told me that he knew Wal-Mart had approached me about purchasing some of the property in Overton Park.

"He said that his legal and real estate firm had negotiated numerous deals with Wal-Mart, and told me he was confident he could get me a better deal than I could get on my own.

"He said that Wal-Mart was very difficult to deal with, and his experience would be invaluable to me.

"I thanked him for his offer, and told him that I would continue to handle my own

Wal-Mart's latest design in North Overton, c. 2007.

negotiations. He strongly advised me against doing so, saying I would be no match for Wal-Mart's real estate team.

"I told him I appreciated his concern, and that I would keep his phone number in case I ran into problems."

From the first conversation McDougal had with Wal-Mart, it took only thirty days until he had a contract from them. They negotiated about two weeks, and had a deal, pending their due diligence clause.

This quick deal didn't fit what he'd heard from others about dealing with the world's largest retailer.

The contract called for a ninety-day due diligence period, where the company would insure that there were no legal or environmental problems with the property.

"The Wal-Mart negotiators had been a pleasure to deal with," McDougal said. "They were professional and courteous."

Over the course of more than twenty five years of buying and selling properties, McDougal had been in many tough negotiations with large and small deals.

"It is not unusual for big companies to try and intimidate the seller in a negotiation," said Delbert. "That didn't happen in this case."

Once the contract was signed, McDougal announced the deal to the public. Immediately, he was flooded with calls from companies who follow Wal-Mart and put in retail stores around them.

"I didn't anticipate how significantly Wal-Mart would change the price of real estate on the east side of this project," McDougal said.

"There are a few businesses located on the perimeter of the Wal-Mart store that will likely stay and realize a great traffic growth. Others will find that the offers for their property will get high enough that they'll choose to sell.

"Businesses were anxious to locate in the vicinity of the new Wal-Mart. We closed three land deals in the first month after the announcement. This was land we expected to hold for several years."

Wal-Mart brought another boost of excitement to the project, and accelerated the development on the east side of Overton Park that borders the downtown area.

McDougal believed that seeing the return of a major retail presence like Wal-Mart to the downtown area would be extremely important to the overall health of the community.

In his view, it would return the vitality back to the central business district, and help bring residential growth back to the area.

PHOTOS BY CHILDRESS PHOTOGRAPHY.

CLOSING THE DEAL

After Delbert signed the Wal-Mart contract, he began discussing changes in the tax increment funding (TIF) projects. The TIF funded streets and infrastructure, paid for out of property tax growth, had begun on the west side of the project. Now, they'd have to expand those upgrades to the east around the proposed Wal-Mart tract.

The City recognized that a Wal-Mart presence would certainly hasten the re-development of the entire downtown area and the eastern part of Lubbock.

"After we had completed our contractual agreement and negotiated a shorter closing date, the due diligence process began," Delbert said.

"Everything went extremely well, until two days before closing when we received a Federal Express from Wal-Mart's attorneys.

"The letter informed me there were thirty eight items that were unacceptable that had to be cleared prior to closing. This triggered some concern as to exactly where Wal-Mart was headed. I felt it was a signal they were going to try to renegotiate our deal.

McDougal spent the next month answering all the questions and awaiting their response.

The contract was delayed again, with more last-minute questions. He began to lose patience.

Wal-Mart incorporated Overton Park's brick and lighting design elements in its Overton Park Super Center.

Delbert had numerous conversations with Tom Hudson during these delays. Hudson explained to him Wal-Mart had to be extremely careful with concerns on environmental issues as the country's largest retailer was highly scrutinized by environmental regulators.

They looked under every rock on the twenty-two acres to ensure that the land was clean and that would not present any problems after closing.

"I was confident there weren't any environmental problems," Delbert said, "Because we had the Texas Commission for Environmental Quality on our property on a continual basis.

"We had a gentlemen from their staff assigned to us, strictly to oversee the area and to ensure that everything was handled properly. With the TCEQ's oversite, I felt extremely comfortable that there weren't any issues with regard to the land."

Finally, the deal closed. Wal-Mart was not trying to bully its way into renegotiating. Delbert deposited the largest check he'd ever seen.

Wal-Mart's entry into Overton Park further raised the national profile of the redevelopment, and jump started commercial activity on the east side. Activity Delbert didn't expect for several years.

"In retrospect, I was extremely impressed with the method the Wal-Mart organization handled their purchasing and negotiations," Delbert reflected.

"The Tom Hudson Company is one of the most professional brokers in the industry, in my opinion. Tom did everything and more that could be asked of a first class representative for Wal-Mart.

"I thought they were overly cautious during the deal, but later learned about costly environmental mitigation they were forced to spend in other deals they'd made. They're cautious because they have to be.

"I have great respect for Wal-Mart and what they mean to the rebuilding of the downtown and northeastern parts of our community, though only once did I ever talk to anyone that was actually on the Wal-Mart payroll."

A NEGOTIATING LESSON

A couple of months prior to the closing as contract negotiations dragged on, one of Delbert's bankers called to tell him they wanted to get a letter from Wal-Mart confirming the latest closing date, even though it was already spelled out in the contract.

McDougal recognized that the lender was feeling a little nervous because the closing kept getting delayed. But Delbert told the banker he would not make that phone call.

"If I would've called Wal-Mart at that moment and asked them for a letter affirming their intention to do what the contract already said, they would've rightly interpreted it as a sign of weakness," Delbert said.

"You never show fear or impatience during negotiations."

CHAPTER 8

OVERTON PARK, 2007 & BEYOND

THE CENTRE OPENS

In July 2005, The Centre at Overton Park held its grand opening. The $30-million project spans two city blocks and contains 277 amenity-rich apartments and more than 20,000 square feet of retail space.

It's stunning interior and exterior design separated it from every other multifamily complex in town. Less than a year after The Centre opened, it was completely occupied.

Residents access all the amenities with state-of-the-art electronic access controls, and can enjoy an e-Café and e-Lounge that are WiFi accessible. The exclusive property also boasts a professionally equipped fitness center, an advanced business center, and two enclosed courtyards with resort-style pool and spa.

Retail shops fill the immense project's first floor. Parking for both shopping and residents is completely hidden inside the perimeter of the building. Shoppers park just a few steps from the retail stores, and residents park on the same level as their apartment.

The complex is striking in appearance, with its majestic Spanish Renaissance design, and sets a proud visual image for the entire development.

Rear view of The Centre.

❖

New properties built in Overton Park.

PHOTOS BY CHILDRESS PHOTOGRAPHY.

❖

The Centre, outside and inside courtyard.

The Shoppes at Overton Park, mixed use residential and retail planned for the 2007 groundbreaking.
COURTESY OF DARYL DUIT.

THE SHOPPES AT OVERTON PARK

The next major announcement came in October 2006, when the Shafer Property Company announced plans to build a $50-million mixed-use shopping center in Overton Park, fronting University Avenue.

The Dallas-based company owns more than fifty shopping centers, and their plans for the Lubbock project also include a 270-unit apartment complex rising above the retail shops.

But the deal was contingent on McDougal's completing his long-planned hotel deal.

"Initially, I planned to develop the shopping center myself," Delbert noted. "But we recognized that we needed the expertise from a retail developer that deals with the national retail market on a daily basis. This process took about a year."

Even after he had an agreement with Shafer, before the deal closed McDougal continued to move forward with his own architectural and engineering plans for the property. This gave Delbert more strength in the negotiations.

"Keeping my own plans moving when I had an apparent deal on the property was a hedge," McDougal said. "This gave me the ability to keep the deal moving forward if the Shafer Company decided to bail on the project. And since they knew what I was doing, it kept the pressure on them to get the deal closed."

In all, McDougal spent $500,000 in architectural and engineering fees developing this property, which he ultimately sold. One might look at it as wasted money, but in the high stakes world of big-time real estate deals, it was both a motivator and an insurance policy. It is not a business for the faint of heart.

McDougal didn't stop his own development just because he had a possible buyer. That is because he learned that a large percentage of deals never close.

"It's easy to get people under contract," Delbert laughed, "but it's harder to close. If you take the approach that you can't afford to walk away from a sale, you'll wind up settling for less.

"In real estate, you've got to have staying power. And you have to negotiate from strength, not weakness.

"More deals fall through than ultimately close. It's crucial to know the buyer, accurately read what's going on, and constantly move forward."

THE HOTEL PROJECT

Numerous parties, including Delbert McDougal, Texas Tech University, the City of Lubbock, and others had tried to package a deal for a first class hotel in Lubbock for the past ten years.

Every few years, word spread that a deal was imminent, but no one had been able to pull it all together.

That didn't stop Delbert from continuing to pursue it. He felt Overton Park was the perfect location for a hotel, with close freeway access and proximity to Tech and downtown.

The hotel was the last big deal to complete his vision for Overton Park.

"Through the years, we tried several different avenues for a hotel," Delbert said. "On more than one occasion we thought we had a deal, then it would fall apart.

"We started with Garfield Traub Development out of Dallas. When talks didn't progress with Garfield, former Tech Board of Regents Chairman Alan White introduced me to John Q. Hammonds, the founder of the Holiday Inn chain.

"Then a deal involving Tech and the Moody Foundation got close enough that they were looking at land sites. But that fell apart due to the changing of the administration at Tech."

After the Moody Foundation deal fell through, Delbert contacted Garfield Traub Development again. They are a national development firm that specializes in hotel projects, and he had a sense that they were the right developer for the Overton Park hotel.

Based in Dallas, Garfield had developed more than twenty-seven million square feet of projects worldwide, but this was its first Texas project. Garfield proposed bringing in 1859 Historic Hotels, a Galveston, Texas-based owner and operator of fine hotels, as the majority owner and operator of the property.

This time, the deal began to gel. The City Council got behind the project, and proposed adding a conference center. They recognized that Lubbock was losing conventions and tourism business, because it didn't have enough first class hotel rooms or conference space.

"The parties agreed to put the privately funded hotel and publicly owned conference center together, Delbert said.

A letter of interest was signed by both sides. Garfield Traub would provide a feasibility study. The City had to work through issues surrounding public ownership of a fifty-thousand-square-foot conference center attached to a private hotel, and what revenues the facility would bring to the community.

The Hotel at Overton Park. Began construction in 2007.
COURTESY OF THE DLR GROUP.

Conference Center attached to The Hotel at Overton Park.
COURTESY OF THE DLR GROUP

Both sides established what they needed. The City needed more space for larger conferences. The developers needed to know how many hotel rooms could be filled through conventions, conferences, tourism, and other local events.

A timeline was established. Delbert worked to keep all parties on course, and helped facilitate working through the problems.

The City Council wanted a known hotel brand, or "flag" for the hotel. But the "flag" came with a cost that might not be offset by increased revenue in the local market.

Delbert argued against spending money for a name brand hotel, preferring to just build a first class hotel with a generic name. He felt people wouldn't decide whether to come to a Lubbock event, based solely on the brand of the hotel. Without the cost of the brand name, more money could be put into the facility.

In January 2007, after four years of negotiations, a deal was in hand.

All the parties gathered in The Centre to announce the $63M project. Garfield Traub and 1859 Historic Hotels committed to put up $46M in debt and equity financing for the land and hotel tower, with funding support from Plains Capital Bank.

The City of Lubbock and a local private foundation are funding construction of the conference center. The City will use increases in the tax valuation from the Overton Park project, and rent payments from the hotel owners to pay debt on the conference center.

The hotel was designed by the DLR Group, a national architecture, engineering, and design services firm. Notable DLR projects include the Overland Park (Kansas) Convention Center and Sheraton Hotel, and the Qwest Center Arena and Convention Center in Omaha, Nebraska. The Lubbock hotel will have 304 rooms and stand 15 stories tall. The 50,000-square-foot convention center includes a 12,000-square-foot ballroom.

After the announcement, Garfield Traub Hospitality Division President Steve Moffett said, "Garfield Traub is honored to be an integral part of the Overton Park re-development. What Delbert McDougal and his team have accomplished is unprecedented in the U.S. Whether a result of vision, hard work, stubbornness, luck, or all of the above, his effort should be both admired and applauded by the citizens of Lubbock and should serve as a model for other blighted and depressed neighborhoods around the country."

"This is the crown jewel of the Overton Park project," Delbert said after the announcement.

"I've never worked so long on a deal that took this many twists and turns, but I wasn't going to let the vision die. Lubbock has needed a first class hotel for a long time, and coupling it

with a much-needed convention center in this location will have a huge impact on the downtown area."

The last major piece of the North Overton project was now in place.

EMINENT DOMAIN

In June 2005, the United States Supreme Court affirmed that local government officials could force property owners to sell for fair compensation, when officials ruled it would benefit the public.

Known as "eminent domain," local governing entities had primarily used the laws to build roads, parks, schools, and other public use facilities. In more contentious cases, cities had used eminent domain to acquire larger tracts of land to help with urban redevelopment, and to facilitate projects to help economic development and tourism.

McDougal assured home owners in North Overton from the outset that he didn't intend to use eminent domain.

But his experience had shown him that eminent domain is needed from time to time.

"I certainly agree with the fundamental right of property ownership," Delbert said. "My company builds and sells homes. No one appreciates the sanctity of a home more than I do.

"But as with most public policy, there are exceptions to every rule. This is especially true in redevelopment of blighted, high crime areas.

"In the case of North Overton, we had to widen streets, reroute drainage, and rezone 325 acres, which would've been impossible without the option of eminent domain.

Surprisingly, out of the more than 900 pieces of property, there were only four issues with owners or tenants that forced McDougal to invoke the eminent domain process. None involved an owner living in his own home.

Two of the properties were vacant lots, one was a business in rented space, and the other

Artist's renditions of the hotel and conference center.
COURTESY OF THE DLR GROUP

was a rented duplex. In no cases were individual homeowners pushed out of their homes. Each of the four properties were eventually settled without the court's action.

"Eminent domain should be used sparingly," Delbert said.

"But I believe that efforts to completely do away with eminent domain are ill-advised political reactions to a few extreme cases of abuse. It will be almost impossible to take care of urban blight without eminent domain as a last resort option.

"I am comfortable that in each of these four cases, a fair deal was reached and our community is going to be better served as a result."

THE FINAL PHASE

Shortly after the hotel announcement, the first single family residences began sprouting up. Deals on all four sides of the project continued to be made, and new construction works its way toward the center of the property.

It would now just be a matter of time, perhaps five to seven years, for the Overton Park project to be completely built out.

"I want to acknowledge and thank City Bank, Plains Capital Bank, and American State Bank for their confidence and financial support throughout the Overton Park project," Delbert said.

In April 2007, McDougal announced a sister project to The Centre. The Suites at Overton Park will be located across the street from the fully occupied luxury apartment complex.

Mary Crites, architect/principal with Lubbock's Parkhill, Smith & Cooper, Inc., had this perspective on the Overton Park project:

"Delbert McDougal has successfully turned his vision into Lubbock's first true mixed-use urban area replete with an in-town traditional neighborhood residential development.

"What was accomplished is unparalleled given the redevelopment challenges but easily rivals components of the 'Celebration' planned community in Florida developed by Walt Disney Corporation, as well as the Addison Circle development in the Dallas-Fort Worth area.

"It is especially fulfilling to have been a part of something that will have such a lasting architectural and economic impact on Lubbock."

Delbert continues to buy and sell properties, and oversee the final stages of his redevelopment. His vision will become his legacy, changing the face of downtown Lubbock forever.

The McDougal family in front of bronze statues of Carolyn and Delbert- a suprise gift from their sons and City Bank. The statues are placed on a sidewalk near the front entrance of Overton Park.

CHAPTER 9

Passing on the Secrets

In more than thirty five years of owning, operating, and managing apartments, McDougal has observed many changes in the industry.

"The most important keys to success," Delbert said, are understanding the market, and hands-on management."

"In nearly every case I've seen where apartments are used as investments for absentee owners, management often wind up squandering money, because it's not their own.

"When people are spending other's money, they often take the easy road, rather than making tough financial decisions."

Carolyn and Delbert in 2007.
PHOTO BY CHILDRESS PHOTOGRAPHY.

Top: Cuyler Lawrence, vice president of special projects.

Above: David Davis, vice president of property maintenance.

McDougal paid $6,500 per unit for his first apartment complex in 1972, and paid nearly $80,000 per unit for his most recent property built in Overton Park.

Bookstore shelves are filled with studies of successful business people. What separates the high achievers from the rest of the pack?

Here is what those closest to Delbert have to say about his business acumen and leadership qualities.

"People look at all the success Delbert has had, but don't really understand what drives him," Carolyn McDougal said.

"Delbert is not driven by acquiring more money. Both of us came from families that had very little money. He likes to do the deals and improve the community. As long as he can pay the bills, he's happy.

"Delbert has many good qualities as a boss. He listens, allows people to be responsible for their areas without micromanaging, and treats all our employees as equals."

Delbert has a very sharp financial mind, and a great memory for numbers. He also has a tremendously positive attitude. He believes that everything he does will work. That's based on experience and know-how, not arrogance.

"When something unexpected forces him to change a strategy, he analyzes his options and changes the plan accordingly," said Marc McDougal.

It's clear that McDougal is also very good at managing in a crisis. Time and again through his career, he's faced down legal and financial crises.

Even though he had many lean financial years, Delbert built a good record with lenders. That's certainly contributed to his ability to manage through rough spots.

"Because of his track record with banks, Delbert has been able to get more money when he needs it," Marc McDougal said.

"Lenders have seen that he does what he says, and that he makes sure that their investments are good deals.

"So when he comes back with a new deal, or asks for more money, they're willing to listen. They don't all say yes every time, but one of them does."

As a manager, Delbert delegates and holds people accountable.

"The one thing that really gets Delbert mad is if you tell him you will do something, then don't do it," Mike McDougal said.

"He has no patience for that. He's fine with people telling him they can't do a project, or they don't know how to do it. He'll either train them, or find someone else who can."

McDougal also values punctuality with the people he works with.

"Delbert starts his meetings on time," Carolyn McDougal said.

"If you walk in five minutes late, you'll wish you hadn't. He'll let you know about it. He feels that everyone's time is important, and that no one should waste their time waiting when an appointment has been scheduled."

Being on time is ingrained in the McDougal corporate culture.

The McDougal Companies held a twentieth anniversary Christmas party in 2002. They rented a local restaurant and told everyone the party started at 6:30.

Restaurants don't normally put a buffet out until people start arriving, so the food will be as fresh as possible. In spite of being advised that people would start arriving early, the restaurant planned for people to start arriving between 6:30 and 7:00.

The restaurant had hosted numerous corporate gatherings, and this was the normal pattern.

At 6:15, everyone arrived. The restaurant folks couldn't believe it.

They'd never seen an entire party show up 15 minutes early.

Delbert always has an underlying sense of humor in his interaction with staff and friends. That sense of fun is also reflected in the corporate culture.

"I hope that we've created a fun and energizing place to work," Carolyn McDougal said.

"We try to create a happy atmosphere. We work hard, and we play hard. We don't want people working here if they're not happy.

"We have people who like what they do, and they like who they're working with. That's why we have employees who have been with us so long."

"Delbert is passionate about his work, and demands excellence from himself and all those around him. Everyone knows where they stand with him.

"And while he may raise his voice when he feels someone hasn't done their best, or accomplished what they said they would, he doesn't berate an employee in a group. If there is a serious issue, it's handled one on one."

Delbert's first employee, Sylvia Vanstory followed Delbert from General Electric.

"I have always been so impressed by how this family works together day in and day out," Sylvia said. "The family enjoys each other. They work together every day, they attend church together, they see each other at night and on weekends, they eat out together, and every year they take a family vacation together.

"When the boys were younger, and the grandchildren were growing up, Delbert always arranged his busy schedule in order to attend school programs and/or other functions for his family. Even if he had an out-of-town guest visiting or investors coming in, he would rearrange his schedule to be there and support his children and grandchildren.

"The McDougals are so wonderful to work for. It was my lucky day when Delbert hired me to come to work for him."

At age seventy, Delbert hasn't slowed down. He still loves his work, and relishes the new challenges and opportunities ahead.

He's also able to travel more and keep that important balance between work and play, employees and family.

"I had to discipline myself to keep work from taking over my family and spiritual life," Delbert said.

"And I had to learn to delegate and trust my managers, so that I can recharge my batteries and enjoy my family when I'm on vacation. If my staff can't do without me when I'm away for a couple of weeks, then I haven't done a good job of training them."

McDougal also encourages his employees to make time for their families, by attending school functions with their children. His company allows employees to use paid time off to attend school functions.

It's also clear that Delbert knows his business. Fortunes are made and lost in the building and development business. McDougal has survived and prospered.

"At City Bank, we do business with a number of developers, said bank President Mike Liner. "A local developer we were financing came to see me one day with bad news. He was in a financial bind in the middle of his project.

"I could see he was in trouble, but didn't know what he could do to get it turned around.

"I called Delbert and asked him to take a look at it. He came in my office and met with both of us. After hearing the developer's story and looking at the plans for a few minutes, he quickly pointed out the problems.

"The developer asked Delbert to join the project, and he agreed to do so. It's now making money for everyone.

"Delbert has taught me a great deal about development, and that makes me a better banker when the next developer comes to me with a project."

It is also clear that community service is integral to Delbert, and to his company.

"In my opinion, Delbert is Mr. Lubbock," said Mike Liner. "He serves on so many boards, and raises so much money for the good of our community.

"I served with Delbert on the University Medical Center Board when he was chairman. UMC is a public hospital, and the current

Left: Sylvia Vanstory, vice president of operations.

Below: David Miler, president, McDougal Construction.

Bottom: Gina Milford, vice president of human resources.

Right: The McDougal ten-year company photo in 1992.

Below: Jeff Lowry, senior vice president of multi-family housing.

Bottom: Julie Berger, vice president of finance.

medical climate has made it tough to stay financially stable.

"As Lubbock's public hospital UMC takes people who come in the door, regardless of their ability to pay. Last year, we provided about $49 million in charity and indigent services and collected $12.4 million in county taxes.

"Delbert brings a common sense business approach to the table, and that is one of the key reasons that UMC has one of the strongest financial positions of any public hospital its size in the state.

McDougal also had an important role for another important Lubbock non-profit. The South Plains Food Bank is a provider of food to those in need locally, and also ships dehydrated foods to people in need all over the world.

For years, the Food Bank struggled year to year for funds, like most non-profits.

"Delbert was asked to chair a capital campaign for the Food Bank," Food Bank President David Weaver said.

"With his leadership, and his personal donation, we raised more than $3 million, and got the Food Bank on solid financial footing.

"And he did this without calling attention to himself. Few people understand Delbert's role in the Food Bank's success."

McDougal was also asked by former Mayor Windy Sitton to chair the Board created to redevelop a closed Air Force base just outside Lubbock.

Reese AFB was phased out in 1997, leaving the community with lost jobs and a base full of aging buildings and potential ground water contamination from years of jet operations.

Under McDougal's guidance, Reese Technology Center was created to position itself as a regional world-class, high technology research, educational training, and business community by generating capital and intellectual wealth.

The first challenge was to get the finances of the operation in order.

"Delbert led a contingent to Washington, D.C., to meet with staff members at the Department of Defense," said Reese Executive Director Eric Williams.

"We were working under a federal plan that allowed closed military bases to eliminate previous debt under very stringent rules and conditions.

"We needed to eliminate an existing long term debt of $3.2 million.

"He got frustrated because the staffers could not give us any answers to his questions.

"Delbert finally asked if there was anyone in the room that could make a decision. When they indicated they could not do so, he suggested they get someone in the room who could.

"After a few phone calls and a short wait, a four star General appeared in the room. We got the decisions we were looking for, and had the tools we needed to retire our debt.

"Reese Technology Center was the first, and for a long time, the only closed military base out of ninety-seven bases in the Base Realignment and Closure act that was debt free and self supporting.

"We couldn't have done it without Delbert McDougal's vision and leadership."

AFTER OVERTON PARK

Even though the major work in Overton Park has been completed, no one around Delbert expected him to slow down.

One of the cities that asked for Delbert's advice on redevelopment was Irving, Texas. Located between Dallas and Fort Worth, Irving is approximately the same size as Lubbock, but has many different challenges.

Irving city leaders made a trip to Lubbock to see his Overton Park redevelopment, and invited him to view their downtown area. The area had some similarities to the Lubbock neighborhood.

Irving had made several attempts to get redevelopment projects started, but they'd fizzled. They wanted to know if Delbert could do the job. He told them he could, and they saw no reason to doubt it.

Rather than retire, Delbert McDougal has launched his next great project, three hundred miles away from Lubbock. There may be skeptics in Irving, but no one in Lubbock has a doubt he'll succeed.

Failure is not an option.

LEAVING A LEGACY FOR HIS SONS

When asked what makes him successful, Delbert McDougal seldom has much of an answer, beyond, "I've just been very fortunate, and I enjoy what I do."

Some may consider Delbert more of a doer than a thinker. But that would be an incomplete assessment of the man.

When McDougal turned sixty, he knew it was time to think about a succession plan for his sons to run the business after he was gone.

"In addition to handling the legal preparation for the transition," Delbert said," I wrote a list of key strategies I felt had been important to what success I've had in business.

Delbert's suggestions to his sons included:
- Take calculated risks based on industry knowledge and growth potential of your market.
- Exercise patience and deal from a position of strength.
- Never be the first to blink. This will lead to a bad deal.
- Stay in businesses that you have a good feeling for. Do not venture into areas you're unfamiliar with unless you've done your homework.
- Behind all appearance of negatives lies positive opportunity.
- Don't be greedy. Share with others and treat others as you would like to be treated.
- Give to charity and to your community.
- To be a winner, you must be a player.
- Position the company for future opportunities.
- Be aware of a changing society and provide those needs.
- Change dictates strategy. Always be willing to adjust.
- Sell outdated properties, and meet the housing needs of the future.
- Be willing to look at other key markets that fit your capabilities.
- Above all, hold your position in your market.
- Be #1 in all areas of business opportunities.
- There will always be another buying opportunity. Be prepared. Be cash strong.
- Stay away from joint ventures unless you remain the key player. Control it or stay out of it!
- Be patient, perceptive, and above all, keep a positive attitude. Good things come from positive thinking.

Delbert and Carolyn McDougal created a successful family business that strives to embody the values taught by their parents. Aided by their sons' considerable contributions, along with a dedicated staff, their companies have achieved great successes by providing quality housing products and real estate services.

"Having the opportunity to build a business with Carolyn, Marc, and Mike has been a great joy," Delbert said.

"I know that not all families can stand to be around each other as much as we do. We're blessed and we know it."

Top: Marc McDougal, president, McDougal Realtors.

Above: Suzanne Comer, vice president of administration.

Afterword

When I approached Delbert McDougal about writing this book in 2003, the Overton Park project was showing early signs of success.

But the jury was out. The project still had its doubters, and new problems seemed to appear every month. A huge tract of land in the middle of town that was a deteriorating slum became a rapidly changing demolition zone. Old houses were knocked down faster than they could be carted off. An arsonist started burning vacant houses. Some questioned the direction of the development. The one constant was Delbert's supreme confidence.

The impact of the Overton Park redevelopment on the way Lubbock looks, its growth patterns, its quality of life and financial growth are immense. The benefits won't be fully measured for at least a decade. It was a monumental undertaking by a visionary developer, his family, and his financial partners.

Developers are essentially gamblers. They take calculated, highly visible risks, and countless fortunes have been won and lost speculating on real estate. Those who enjoy success in this field learn to never show fear or doubt.

During the course of many interviews about his company, the only time McDougal ever acknowledged stress was when he told me nothing makes him angrier than for an employee to use the excuse that he or she was 'stressed out' when trying to justify not completing a project.

"I'll tell you what stress is," McDougal said. "Stress is waking up and knowing you have to meet a $50,000 payroll by the end of the day with nothing in the bank."

I have no doubt McDougal felt the stress as he walked in to his banker's office that morning, but am equally certain he didn't show it. He knew he was going to get the loan and meet his payroll. If by chance he was turned down, he knew he'd get it at the next bank.

Failure was not an option.

My goal in telling the Horatio Alger story of the McDougal Companies was to give the reader a glimpse inside the mind of a hugely successful entrepreneur, from the company's rocky beginning through the crowning achievement of a massive and risky redevelopment project.

It is also the story of a very tight family, and how they interact with each other as business people. I've observed and worked in family businesses, but have never seen one live and work together like the McDougals.

Delbert, Carolyn, Marc, & Mike are in almost constant touch with each other every day. They eat lunch and dinner as a group several times a week, go to the same church, attend sporting events, and take long vacations together.

Even though I agreed that Delbert would have the final approval of anything I published in this book, it took a great deal of trust for him and all the family to divulge so much privileged information to me. Every question I asked was answered.

Yet the only information Delbert insisted I remove from the manuscript were the names of people he feared might be needlessly embarrassed by some element of the story.

It is impossible to imagine this company's success without Carolyn McDougal's steadying relationship in their business. Delbert is the first to credit the importance of Carolyn's work in managing, decorating, and leasing apartments, a core element of their business. To this day, no one in the company can lease apartments as successfully as Carolyn.

One of the best measures of character in business is how an owner treats his employees. In my interviews with long-term staff, I offered the opportunity to speak off the record. Instead, I found a refreshing eagerness to tell the many qualities of their boss.

They praised Delbert as a strong leader with high expectations who cares about his employees, customers, and community. He demands excellence, but will also quietly help out an employee in a crisis.

It is impossible for me to adequately describe one of Delbert's key qualities, his contagious optimism. He picks up the energy in a room when he walks in, and communicates with an underlying sense of humor, even in a heated disagreement.

More importantly, he has the ability to transfer his own drive for success to others.

In the highly acclaimed book *Good to Great* (2001, HarperCollins), Jim Collins describes what he calls the "Level 5 Executive":

> Level 5 leaders channel their ego needs away from themselves and into the larger goal of building a great company. It's not that Level 5 leaders have no ego or self-interest. Indeed, they are incredibly ambitious – but their ambition is first and foremost for the institution, not themselves.

I believe that description clearly fits Delbert McDougal. He is not driven by acquiring money, nor the ostentatious show of wealth.

His interest is in making the next deal, and in building a company of people who share in its success. His work has touched many lives, and left a legacy for generations.

I am deeply grateful for the trust and constant encouragement of the McDougal family in sharing their stories for this book.

I also thank George and Nawanna Privett for their insights and suggestions on the manuscript. Very special thanks go to Judy Privett, a fine editor and the great love of my life.

Tony Privett
July 2007

McDougal Companies twenty-fifth anniversary photograph.
PHOTO BY CHILDRESS PHOTOGRAPHY.

Acknowledgments

Delbert McDougal recognizes the many companies, organizations, and individuals whose work helped make the Overton Park redevelopment a success:

Acordia West Texas Agency
American State Bank
Atmos Energy
AT&T
Blosser Appraisal
Childress Photography
City Bank Lubbock
City of Lubbock
Dinerstein Companies
Dyess Peterson Testing Laboratory Inc.
Grimes And Associates
McClendon Law Firm
High Plains Underground Water District
Howard, Cunningham & Houchin
Hugo Reed And Associates Inc
Humphreys & Partners Architects
Lubbock Power & Light & Water
Lubbock County
Lubbock County Hospital District
Matthews Backhoe Inc.
Parkhill, Smith, & Cooper
Plains Capital Bank
Suddenlink
Texas Commission On Environmental Quality
Texas Department Of Health & Human Services
Tony Privett Communications
Texas Department Of Housing & Community Affairs
VanCo, Inc.
Western Title Company
West Texas Abatement
Xcel Energy

"I thank all of you for your great work and support, along with the fine staff of the McDougal Companies."

Delbert McDougal
July 2007